REPORT ON THE HISTORICAL RECORD OF U.S. GOVERNMENT INVOLVEMENT WITH UNIDENTIFIED ANOMALOUS PHENOMENA (UAP) VOLUME 1

ALL-DOMAIN ANOMALY RESOLUTION OFFICE

NIMBLE BOOKS LLC: THE AI LAB FOR BOOK-LOVERS

~ FRED ZIMMERMAN, EDITOR ~

Humans and AI making books richer, more diverse, and more surprising.

PUBLISHING INFORMATION

(c) 2024 Nimble Books LLC
ISBN: 978-1-60888-270-0

AI-GENERATED KEYWORD PHRASES

Project SAUCER; Project SIGN; Project GRUDGE; Project TWINKLE; Project BEAR; CIA Special Study Group; The Robertson Panel; The Durant Report; Project BLUE BOOK; CIA Evaluation of UFOs; O'Brien Committee; U.S. Air Force; Office of the Director of National Intelligence; Department of Defense; RQ-170 Sentinel.

PUBLISHER'S NOTES

This annotated edition illustrates the capabilities of the AI Lab for Book-Lovers to add context and ease-of-use to manuscripts. It includes several types of abstracts, building from simplest to more complex: TLDR (one word), ELI5, TLDR (vanilla), Scientific Style, and Action Items; essays to increase viewpoint diversity, such as Grounds for Dissent, Red Team Critique, and MAGA Perspective; and Notable Passages and Nutshell Summaries for each page.

ANNOTATIONS

ABSTRACTS

TL;DR (ONE WORD)

UFOs.

EXPLAIN IT TO ME LIKE I'M FIVE YEARS OLD

This document talks about different projects and reports related to UFOs and alien spacecraft. It says that a sample of a crashed spacecraft was actually made on Earth and not from outer space. It also mentions that there is no evidence of the government trying to copy alien technology, and most claims about this are not true. The document also includes links to reports from the U.S. Air Force and other government agencies about UFO sightings and investigations.

TL;DR (VANILLA)

The document discusses various UFO-related projects and reports, including Project SAUCER, Project SIGN, Project GRUDGE, Project TWINKLE, Project BEAR, Project BLUE BOOK, and more. It also mentions the CIA Special Study Group, the Robertson Panel, the Durant Report, and the O'Brien Committee. The document refutes claims of UAP reverse-engineering programs and states that a sample from an alleged crashed off-world spacecraft is a terrestrial alloy. Additionally, it highlights that all authentic programs have been properly reported to Congress.

SCIENTIFIC STYLE

The provided information highlights various projects and committees established by the U.S. government related to UFOs and extraterrestrial phenomena, such as Project SAUCER, SIGN, GRUDGE, TWINKLE, BEAR, and BLUE BOOK. It also addresses the investigation of alleged extraterrestrial spacecraft samples, concluding that they are terrestrial in origin. The document emphasizes that none of the programs were related to UAP reverse-engineering and disputes claims made by interviewees. Additionally, it references official reports from the U.S. Air Force, the Department of Defense, and the Office of the Director of National Intelligence regarding unidentified aerial phenomena.

ACTION ITEMS

The document provides a timeline of various projects and committees related to UFOs and UAPs, including Project SAUCER, Project SIGN, Project GRUDGE, Project TWINKLE, Project BEAR, Project BLUE BOOK, and more.

It mentions that there is no evidence for UAP reverse-engineering programs and that all authentic programs have been properly reported to Congress.

The document also discusses the investigation of an alleged crashed off-world spacecraft sample, which was determined to be a terrestrial alloy.

VIEWPOINTS

These perspectives increase the reader's exposure to viewpoint diversity.

GROUNDS FOR DISSENT

A member of the organization responsible for this document may have principled, substantive reasons to dissent from this report because they may believe that the conclusion regarding the alleged extraterrestrial spacecraft sample is inaccurate. They may argue that the methods used to analyze the sample were flawed or incomplete, leading to a false determination of its terrestrial origin. Additionally, they may disagree with the assertion that none of the programs mentioned by interviewees are UAP reverse-engineering programs, believing that there is evidence to suggest otherwise. They may also question the thoroughness of the investigation conducted by AARO, arguing that key evidence or witnesses were overlooked or dismissed without proper consideration. Overall, the dissenting member may feel that the report is biased or incomplete in its analysis, leading to a lack of confidence in its findings.

RED TEAM CRITIQUE

Based on the selected sentences from the document, it appears that the document is focused on debunking claims of UAP reverse-engineering programs and discrediting the narratives provided by interviewees. The document asserts that a sample from an alleged crashed off-world spacecraft is actually a terrestrial alloy and not of extraterrestrial origin. It also states that all authentic programs related to UAPs have been properly reported to Congress. The document emphasizes the lack of evidence for USG reverse-engineering narratives and highlights the ability to disprove many claims made by interviewees.

From a red team perspective, the document seems to be aimed at dismissing conspiracy theories and debunking myths surrounding UAPs, alien technology, and government cover-ups. It appears to be attempting to reassure the public that there is no evidence of extraterrestrial spacecraft being reverse-engineered by the US government, and that any claims suggesting otherwise are unfounded. However, the document may be criticized for potentially overlooking or dismissing legitimate concerns or evidence related to UAPs, and for presenting a one-sided perspective without considering alternative viewpoints or interpretations of the data. Additionally, the document may be questioned for its reliance on official government statements and reports, which could be biased or incomplete.

MAGA PERSPECTIVE

The document clearly outlines a series of government projects related to UFOs, showing that the government has been involved in studying and analyzing these phenomena for decades. However, the fact that none of these projects are specifically mentioned as UAP reverse-engineering programs is suspicious. It is clear that the government is hiding something and not being transparent with the American people. The denial of any evidence for reverse-engineering and the disproof of many claims by interviewees only serves to further the skepticism and distrust in the government's narrative.

Additionally, the report mentions that all authentic programs have been properly reported to Congress, but we know that the government has a history of hiding information and conducting covert operations without congressional oversight. The fact that these programs have been kept under wraps for so long is concerning and raises questions about what else the government may be hiding from the public. The lack of transparency and accountability in these UFO projects is a clear violation of the trust that the American people have placed in their government.

Furthermore, the mention of a sample from an alleged crashed off-world spacecraft being a terrestrial alloy rather than off-world technology is suspicious. This could be a deliberate attempt by the government to cover up any evidence of extraterrestrial visitation and maintain their control over the narrative. It is clear that there is a concerted effort to discredit any claims of UFO sightings or encounters in order to maintain the status quo and prevent any disruption to the government's power and authority.

Overall, the document provides a glimpse into the secretive world of government UFO projects and raises serious concerns about the level of transparency and honesty from the government. The denial of any evidence for reverse-engineering, the lack of transparency in reporting to Congress, and the discrediting of claims by interviewees all point to a deliberate effort to maintain control over the narrative and prevent the truth from coming out. The American people deserve to know the full extent of government involvement in UFO research and the true nature of these phenomena, rather than being fed half-truths and misinformation.

PAGE-BY-PAGE SUMMARIES

BODY-13   Research conducted by AARO reveals the existence of approximately two dozen USG investigative efforts involving UFOs/UAP since 1945, including Projects SAUCER/SIGN, GRUDGE, and BLUE BOOK, as well as short-term projects and reviews such as the CIA-sponsored Study Group and the Durant Report.

BODY-14   Project SAUCER and Project SIGN investigated UFO sightings for national security, with no evidence of extraterrestrial technology found. Project SIGN evaluated 243 sightings, concluding most were misinterpretations or hoaxes, but did not rule out extraterrestrial phenomena. A report claiming UFOs were interplanetary was rejected.

BODY-15   Project GRUDGE investigated UFO sightings, found no threat to national security, and recommended downsizing to alleviate public anxiety. Project TWINKLE failed to capture images of "green fireballs" in Nevada and New Mexico. Reestablished in 1951, Project GRUDGE aimed to correct past mistakes and avoid wild speculation.

BODY-16   Project GRUDGE under Capt Ruppelt aimed for objectivity by allowing an "unknown" category for UFO cases. Project BEAR provided scientific support and statistical analysis, concluding that all cases were explainable and not beyond present scientific knowledge. The CIA Special Study Group found most reports explainable and not of Soviet or extraterrestrial origin.

BODY-17   The page discusses the CIA's concern over UFO sightings in the 1950s, leading to the establishment of the Robertson Panel to review the evidence. The panel concluded that most sightings had ordinary explanations and posed no threat to national security, but were concerned about potential mass hysteria.

BODY-18   Project BLUE BOOK was a USAF investigation into UFO sightings from 1952-1969, led by various officers and J. Allen Hynek. It categorized sightings as identified, insufficient data, or unidentified, with explanations including astronomical sightings, balloons, aircraft, and afterburners. The project was terminated in 1969 by Secretary of the Air Force Robert C. Seamans, Jr.

BODY-19   Research on Project BLUE BOOK by AARO and the US National Archives found no evidence of UFOs as a threat to national security or of extraterrestrial origin. CIA and O'Brien Committee evaluations reached similar conclusions, recommending further academic research. The Condon Report supported these findings.

BODY-20   Panel concludes that UFO studies do not advance scientific knowledge, dismisses physical evidence claims as ordinary, and debunks Frank Edwards' claims of recovered UFO fragments. NAS panel assesses Condon Report without investigating UFO reports.

BODY-21   Government investigations into UFOs, including the Roswell incident, did not find evidence of alien spacecraft or cover-ups. President Clinton and the USAF conducted inquiries and released reports debunking the conspiracy theories.

BODY-22   The page discusses the Roswell incident, debunking claims of aliens and UFOs by attributing recovered materials to a U.S. Army Air Force balloon program. It also outlines the Advanced Aerospace Weapons System Application Program (AAWSAP) and Advanced Aerospace Threat Identification Program (AATIP) funded by the DIA to assess foreign aerospace threats.

BODY-23   The AAWSAP/AATIP program investigated UFO/UAP phenomena, including unconventional propulsion and materials, but was terminated in 2012 due to concerns about the project. Research included reviewing cases, setting up laboratories, and exploring paranormal activities. The program also proposed a public relations campaign to influence public debate on extraterrestrial visitations.

BODY-24   Establishment of UAPTF to study unidentified aerial phenomena, leading to improved reporting and identification of potential threats. Preliminary assessment highlights challenges in understanding nature and intent of UAP, emphasizing need for standardized reporting and analysis. AOIMSG succeeds UAPTF to synchronize efforts in identifying and managing airborne objects.

BODY-25   NASA established the UAP Independent Study Team to examine UAP from a scientific perspective, focusing on data and tools. AARO, formerly AOIMSG, was expanded to address UAP issues, providing reports to Congress based on data collected.

BODY-26   AARO Director reports no evidence of extraterrestrial technology in investigated cases. Various foreign investigatory efforts, including Stanford University and Canadian projects, have not found convincing evidence of UFO/UAP of extraterrestrial origin. French government sponsored programs also found no definitive results.

BODY-27   Various investigations, including USG, foreign, and academic efforts, found no evidence of extraterrestrial origin in UAP reports. Most cases were explained as ordinary objects or natural phenomena, with unresolved cases due to lack of data and resource constraints. USG proposals aimed to debunk UFO reports to prevent mass hysteria.

BODY-28   AARO conducted interviews with individuals claiming USG involvement in hidden UAP programs, categorizing them into three tiers. Two main narratives emerged, alleging possession and testing of off-world technology since 1964, with claims of extraterrestrial spacecraft and materials. No empirical evidence was found to support these claims.

BODY-29   Various interviewees shared accounts of encounters with extraterrestrial spacecraft and beings, as well as involvement in secret government studies and projects related to UFOs. Claims include reverse-engineering alien technology, witnessing UFOs at military facilities, and loading containers onto extraterrestrial spacecraft.

BODY-30   Investigation into UAP sightings near nuclear facilities and claims of disruptions to ICBM operations. No official UAP Nondisclosure Agreements found, standard NDA language includes penalties for disclosing classified information.

BODY-31   Former CIA official denies involvement in alleged movement of material from a UAP crash. Special National Intelligence Estimate from 1961 on UFOs deemed inauthentic. Misunderstanding likely in account of aliens observing material test.

BODY-32   Former military member denies touching extraterrestrial spacecraft, correlates strange sighting with authentic USG program, extraterrestrial disclosure study not White House-sponsored, aerospace companies deny involvement, alleged alien spacecraft material found to be ordinary metal alloy.

BODY-33   AARO investigated metallic material, found it to be terrestrial, and debunked claims of off-world technology reverse-engineering. They also looked into historical nuclear-related UAP cases and named USG sensitive programs, finding no evidence of capturing or reverse-engineering extraterrestrial technology.

BODY-34   AARO investigated sensitive programs, found a private program mistaken for a USG program, and uncovered details about KONA BLUE, a proposed UAP recovery and reverse-engineering program linked to AAWSAP/AATIP.

BODY-35   Rejected proposal for a Special Access Program to investigate UAP technologies, lacking merit and evidence. Unnecessary expansion of IC program for UAP reverse-engineering mission disestablished due to lack of activity and merit. No empirical evidence found for UAP investigatory efforts since 1945.

NOTABLE PASSAGES

BODY-3   *"Former CIA Official Involvement in Movement of Alleged Material Recovered from a UAP Crash Denied on the Record."*

BODY-6   *"A consistent theme in popular culture involves a particularly persistent narrative that the USG—or a secretive organization within it—recovered several off-world spacecraft and extraterrestrial biological remains, that it operates a program or programs to reverse engineer the recovered technology, and that it has conspired since the 1940s to keep this effort hidden from the United States Congress and the American public."*

BODY-7   *"AARO found no evidence that any USG investigation, academic-sponsored research, or official review panel has confirmed that any sighting of a UAP represented extraterrestrial technology. All investigative efforts, at all levels of classification, concluded that most sightings were ordinary objects and phenomena and the result of misidentification. Although not the focus of this report, it is worthwhile to note that all official foreign UAP investigatory efforts to date have reached the same general conclusions as USG investigations."*

BODY-9   *AARO assesses that the inaccurate claim that the USG is reverse-engineering extraterrestrial technology and is hiding it from Congress is, in large part, the result of circular reporting from a group of individuals who believe this to be the case, despite the lack of any evidence. AARO notes that although claims that the USG has recovered and hidden spacecraft date back to the 1940s and 1950s, more modern instances of these claims largely stem from a consistent group of individuals who have been involved in various UAP-related endeavors since at least 2009.*

BODY-10   *Several factors—domestic and international—most likely influenced sightings, reports, and the belief by some individuals that there is sufficient proof that some UAP represent extraterrestrial technology.*

BODY-11   *"It is understandable how observers unfamiliar with these programs could mistake sightings of these new technologies as something extraordinary, even other-worldly."*

BODY-12   *"Some literature suggests individual accounts can be unreliable as they are subject to a person's interpretation of sensory data through the filter of their experiences, beliefs, or state of mind during the event. A person who reports a case might be credible, in that they believe the elements of their account to be accurate. However, their reliability, which is their ability to accurately interpret events—as well as to recall and convey those events due to a range of factors—is altogether different from their inherent sincerity."*

BODY-13   *AARO reviewed official USG efforts involving UFOs/UAP since 1945. This research revealed the existence of approximately two dozen separate investigative efforts, depending on how they are counted. These efforts ranged from formal, distinct programs employing a dedicated staff with some measure of longevity including: Projects SAUCER/SIGN, GRUDGE, and BLUE BOOK, the DoD UAP Task Force (UAPTF) led by the U.S. Navy (USN), the Airborne Object Identification and Management Synchronization Group (AOIMSG), and the All-domain Anomaly Resolution Office (AARO). There were also short-term projects that supported some of these established programs including: Projects TWINKLE and BEAR and*

BODY-14   *"Although the historical account is unsubstantiated and derived from only one source, Project SIGN staff in late July 1948 allegedly drafted, signed, and sent a* report ("Estimate of the Situation") up the military chain for approval. This report allegedly concluded that UFOs were "interplanetary" in origin, but it was rejected by USAF Chief of Staff General Hoyt S. Vandenberg as lacking proof."

BODY-16   No evidence of extraterrestrial origin of UFO/UAP were discovered.

BODY-17   Chadwell urged action because he was convinced that "something was going on that must have immediate attention," and that "sightings of unexplained objects at great altitudes and traveling at high speeds in the vicinity of major U.S. defense installations are of such nature that they are not attributable to natural phenomena or known types of aerial vehicles."

BODY-19   "No UFO reported, investigated, and evaluated by the USAF demonstrated any indication of a threat to national security. There was no evidence submitted to, or discovered by, the USAF that sightings represented technological developments or principles beyond the range of then-present day scientific knowledge. There was no evidence indicating that sightings categorized as unidentified are 'extraterrestrial vehicles.' Of the 12,618 sightings in Project BLUE BOOK's holdings, 701 were categorized as unidentified and never solved."

BODY-20   "Our general conclusion is that nothing has come from the study of UFOs in the past 21 years that has added to scientific knowledge. Careful consideration of the record as it is available to us leads us to conclude that further extensive study of UFOs probably cannot be justified in the expectation that science will be advanced thereby."

BODY-21   President Clinton said, "As far as I know, an alien spacecraft did not crash in Roswell, New Mexico, in 1947...if the USAF did recover alien bodies, they didn't tell me about it...and I want to know."

BODY-22   The alleged "alien" bodies reported by some in the New Mexico desert were test dummies that were carried aloft by U.S. Army Air Force high-altitude balloons for scientific research.

BODY-23   "The organization also planned to hire psychics to study 'inter-dimensional phenomena' believed to frequently appear at that location."

BODY-24   The preliminary assessment concluded that: (1) the limited amount of high-quality reporting on UAP hampers the ability to draw firm conclusions about their nature or intent; (2) in a limited number of incidents, UAP reportedly appeared to exhibit unusual flight characteristics; although those observations could be the result of sensor errors, spoofing, or observer misperception and require additional rigorous analysis; (3) there are probably multiple types of UAP requiring different explanations based on the range of appearances and behaviors described in the available reporting; (4) UAP may pose airspace safety issues and a challenge to U.S. national security; and (5) consistent consolidation of reports from across the USG, standardized reporting, increased collection and analysis, and

BODY-25   The report stated that there was a total of 510 UAP reports as of August 30, 2022. This included the 144 UAP reports covered during the 17 years of reporting included in the ODNI's preliminary assessment, as well as 247 new reports and 119 reports that subsequently were discovered or reported.

BODY-26   "Stanford University's Sturrock Panel (1998) found no convincing evidence for the extraterrestrial origin of UFO/UAP."

BODY-27   "The lack of actionable, researchable data—specifically the lack of speed, altitude, and size of reported UAP—combined with resource constraints, high volumes of cases, and perceived differing levels of support from USG officials were factors in all investigative efforts."

BODY-28   *The primary narrative alleges that the USG and industry partners are in possession of and are testing off-world technology that has been concealed from congressional oversight and the world since approximately 1964, and possibly since 1947, if the Roswell events are included. The narrative asserts that this UAP program possesses as many as 12 extraterrestrial spacecraft.*

BODY-30   *"Specifically, they said the ICBM launch control facilities went offline or experienced total power failure. Additionally, one interviewee and a USAF videographer claimed to have observed and recorded a UAP destroying an ICBM loaded with a "dummy" warhead, mid-flight."*

BODY-32   *"Sample of Alleged Alien Spacecraft is an Ordinary, Terrestrial, Metal Alloy*

AARO learned through an interviewee that a private sector organization claimed to have in its possession material from an extraterrestrial craft recovered from a crash at an unknown location from the 1940s or 1950s. The organization claimed that the material had the potential to act as a THz frequency waveguide, and therefore, could exhibit "anti-gravity" and "mass reduction" properties under the appropriate conditions. The organization that owned the material negotiated an agreement in 2019 with the U.S. Army to analyze the samples. With permission from the stakeholders, AARO acquired this sample to conduct more in-depth analyses."

BODY-33   *"AARO concludes many of these programs represent authentic, current and former sensitive, national security programs, but none of these programs have been involved with capturing, recovering, or reverse-engineering off-world technology or material."*

BODY-34   *"When DIA cancelled this program, its supporters proposed to DHS that they create and fund a new version of AAWSAP/AATIP under a SAP. This proposal, codenamed KONA BLUE, would restart UAP investigations, paranormal research (including alleged "human consciousness anomalies") and reverse-engineer any recovered off-world spacecraft that they hoped to acquire."*

BODY-35   *"KONA BLUE's advocates were convinced that the USG was hiding UAP technologies. They believed that creating this program under DHS would allow all of the technology and knowledge of these alleged programs to be moved under the KONA BLUE program. The program would provide a security and governing structure where it could be monitored properly by congressional oversight committees."*

BODY-36   *"AARO assesses that the incidents of UAP sightings reported to USG organizations, the claims that some constitute extraterrestrial craft, and the claims that the USG has secured and is experimenting on alien technology, most likely are the result of a range of cultural, political, and technological factors. AARO bases this conclusion on the aggregate findings of all USG investigations to date, the misinterpretation of all reported named sensitive programs, the lack of empirical evidence to support the USG reverse-engineering narrative, and AARO's assessment that the piece of metal alleged to be recovered from an alien spacecraft in the late 1940s is ordinary, of terrestrial origin, and possesses no exceptional qualities."*

BODY-37   *"Although many UAP/UFO cases remain unsolved, based on the lack of evidence of the extraterrestrial origin of even one UAP report and the assessment that all resolved cases to date have ordinary explanations, AARO assess sightings and claims of extraterrestrial visitations have been influenced by a range of factors."*

BODY-38   *"There is a conviction among some Americans that the USG has conducted a deception operation to conceal the fact that it has recovered extraterrestrial* spacecraft and alien beings as well as systematically exploited and reverse-engineered extraterrestrial technology."

BODY-39   "However, we assess that some portion of these misidentifications almost certainly were a result of the surge in new technologies that observers would have understandably reported as UFOs."

BODY-40   The secrecy surrounding the Manhattan Project and the establishment of several other national laboratories, such as Los Alamos National Laboratories, Lawrence Livermore National Laboratory, Sandia National Laboratories, Pacific Northwest National Laboratory, and Oak Ridge National Laboratory to support this effort probably contributed to the spike in reported UAP.

BODY-41   "President Eisenhower approved this CIA-led program to develop a successor to the U-2 spy plane in 1958, which became fully operational in 1965. The U-2's successor, the A-12 OXCART sustained a speed of Mach 3.2 at 90,000 feet altitude."

BODY-42   "The United States was the first nation to deliver a reconnaissance satellite to space. This electronic intelligence (ELINT) satellite was developed by the Naval Research Laboratory in early 1958 under the code name "TATTLETALE" with the mission of intercepting Soviet radar signals."

BODY-43   "At the initiative of President Ronald Reagan, the Strategic Defense Initiative Organization was established in 1984 to explore a multi-layered strategic defense against ballistic missiles; this program involved research into space-based and ground-based systems including laser and interceptor missiles."

BODY-44   "Reaper General Atomics Aeronautical Systems, Inc. also built the MQ-9 Reaper—a newer, larger version of the MQ-1 Predator UAV. This platform is faster, equipped with more advanced sensors, can carry more munitions than the Predator, and can be easily tailored with a variety of mission-specific capabilities."

BODY-45   To date, AARO has not discovered any empirical evidence that any sighting of a UAP represented off-world technology or the existence a classified program that had not been properly reported to Congress. Investigative efforts determined that most sightings were the result of misidentification of ordinary objects and phenomena. Although many UAP reports remain unsolved, AARO assesses that if additional, quality data were available, most of these cases also could be identified and resolved as ordinary objects or phenomena."

THE DEPARTMENT OF DEFENSE
ALL-DOMAIN ANOMALY RESOLUTION OFFICE

Report on the Historical Record of U.S. Government Involvement with Unidentified Anomalous Phenomena (UAP)

Volume I

February 2024

1

Table of Contents

3

4

5

SECTION I: Introduction

This report represents Volume I of the All-domain Anomaly Resolution Office's (AARO) Historical Record Report (HR2) which reviews the record of the United States Government (USG) pertaining to unidentified anomalous phenomena (UAP). In completing this report, AARO reviewed all official USG investigatory efforts since 1945, researched classified and unclassified archives, conducted approximately 30 interviews, and partnered with Intelligence Community (IC) and Department of Defense (DoD) officials responsible for controlled and special access program oversight, respectively. AARO will publish Volume II in accordance with the date established in Section 6802 of the National Defense Authorization Act for Fiscal Year 2023 (FY23); Volume II will provide analysis of information acquired by AARO after the date of the publication of Volume I.

Since 1945, the USG has funded and supported UAP investigations with the goal of determining whether UAP represented a flight safety risk, technological leaps by competitor nations, or evidence of off-world technology under intelligent control. These investigations were managed and implemented by a range of experts, scientists, academics, military, and intelligence officials under differing leaders—all of whom held their own perspectives that led them to particular conclusions on the origins of UAP. However, they all had in common the belief that UAP represented an unknown and, therefore, theoretically posed a potential threat of an indeterminate nature.

AARO's mission is similar to that of these earlier organizations. AARO methodology applies both the scientific method and intelligence analysis tradecraft to identify and help mitigate risks UAP may pose to domain safety and to discover, characterize, and attribute potential competitor technological systems.

A consistent theme in popular culture involves a particularly persistent narrative that the USG—or a secretive organization within it—recovered several off-world spacecraft and extraterrestrial biological remains, that it operates a program or programs to reverse engineer the recovered technology, and that it has conspired since the 1940s to keep this effort hidden from the United States Congress and the American public.

AARO recognizes that many people sincerely hold versions of these beliefs which are based on their perception of past experiences, the experiences of others whom they trust, or media and online outlets they believe to be sources of credible and verifiable information. The proliferation of television programs, books, movies, and the vast amount of internet and social media content centered on UAP-related topics most likely has influenced the public conversation on this topic, and reinforced these beliefs within some sections of the population.

The goal of this report is not to prove or disprove any particular belief set, but rather to use a rigorous analytic and scientific approach to investigate past USG-sponsored UAP investigation efforts and the claims made by interviewees that the USG and various contractors have recovered and are hiding off-world technology and biological material. AARO has approached this project with the widest possible aperture, thoroughly investigating these

6

assertions and claims without any particular pre-conceived conclusion or hypothesis. AARO is committed to reaching conclusions based on empirical evidence.

Lastly, AARO thanks all participants in this review who made this report possible, to include the interviewees who came forward with information.

SECTION II: Executive Summary

AARO found no evidence that any USG investigation, academic-sponsored research, or official review panel has confirmed that any sighting of a UAP represented extraterrestrial technology. All investigative efforts, at all levels of classification, concluded that most sightings were ordinary objects and phenomena and the result of misidentification. Although not the focus of this report, it is worthwhile to note that all official foreign UAP investigatory efforts to date have reached the same general conclusions as USG investigations.

- Although many UAP reports remain unsolved or unidentified, AARO assesses that if more and better quality data were available, most of these cases also could be identified and resolved as ordinary objects or phenomena. Sensors and visual observations are imperfect; the vast majority of cases lack actionable data or the data available is limited or of poor quality.

- Resources and staffing for these programs largely have been irregular and sporadic, challenging investigatory efforts and hindering effective knowledge transfer.

- The vast majority of reports almost certainly are the result of misidentification and a direct consequence of the lack of domain awareness; there is a direct correlation between the amount and quality of available information on a case with the ability to conclusively resolve it.

AARO found no empirical evidence for claims that the USG and private companies have been reverse-engineering extraterrestrial technology. AARO determined, based on all information provided to date, that claims involving specific people, known locations, technological tests, and documents allegedly involved in or related to the reverse-engineering of extraterrestrial technology, are inaccurate. Additional claims will be addressed in Volume II. AARO successfully located the USG and industry programs, officials, companies, executives, and documents identified by interviewees. In many cases, the interviewees named authentic USG classified programs well-known and understood to those appropriately accessed to them in the Executive Branch and Legislative Branch; however, the interviewees mistakenly associated these authentic USG programs with alien and extraterrestrial activity. AARO has reached the following, high confidence conclusions related to:

- **UAP Nondisclosure Agreements (NDA):** AARO has found no evidence of any authentic UAP-related NDA or other evidence threatening death or violence for disclosing UAP information.

7

- **A CIA Official Allegedly Managed UAP Experimentation:** The named, former CIA official was not involved in the movement of extraterrestrial technology. The same former CIA officer signed a memo rejecting a claim made by interviewees that he managed the movement of and experimentation on off-world technology.

- **Alleged UAP Intelligence Community Document:** An alleged 1961 Special National Intelligence Estimate that was "leaked" to online sources and suggests the extraterrestrial nature of "UFOs," is inauthentic.

- **"Aliens" Present During a DoD Technology Test:** AARO reviewed information related to an account of an interviewee overhearing a conversation about a technology test at a military base where "aliens" allegedly were observing, and AARO judges that the interviewee misunderstood the conversation.

- **Claim That a Military Officer Touched an Off-World Craft:** An interviewee claim that a named former military officer explained in detail how he physically touched an extraterrestrial spacecraft is inaccurate. The claim was denied on the record by the named former officer who recounted a story of when he touched an F-117 Nighthawk stealth fighter that could have been misconstrued by the interviewee, though the named former officer does not recall having this conversation with the interviewee.

- **Test of Off-World Technology:** An interviewee claim that he witnessed what he believed to be the testing of extraterrestrial technology at a USG facility almost certainly was an observation of an authentic, non-UAP-related, technology test that strongly correlated in time, location, and description provided in the interviewee's account.

- **UAP Disclosure Study:** Interviewees' claims that between 2004 and 2007 the White House requested a research institute in Virginia study the theoretical societal impacts of disclosing that UAP are extraterrestrial in origin; AARO confirmed the study was conducted, but it was not requested by the White House.

- **Named Companies Allegedly Experimenting on Alien Technology:** AARO has found no evidence that U.S. companies ever possessed off-world technology. The executives, scientists, and chief technology officers of the companies named by interviewees met with the Director of AARO and denied on the record that they have ever recovered, possessed, or engaged in reverse-engineering of extraterrestrial technology.

- **Experimentation on Alleged Extraterrestrial Spacecraft Sample:** AARO has concluded that a sample from an alleged crashed off-world spacecraft that AARO acquired from a private UAP investigating organization and the U.S. Army is a manufactured, terrestrial alloy and does not represent off-world technology or possess any exceptional qualities. The sample is primarily composed of magnesium, zinc, and bismuth with some other trace elements, such as lead. This assessment was based on its materials characterization.

AARO assesses that all of the named and described alleged hidden UAP reverse-engineering programs provided by interviewees either do not exist; are misidentified authentic, highly sensitive national security programs that are not related to extraterrestrial technology exploitation; or resolve to an unwarranted and disestablished program. AARO created a secure process in partnership with the highest-level security officials within the DoD, IC, and other organizations to research and investigate these programs; AARO was granted full, unrestricted access by all organizations. It is important to note that none of the interviewees had firsthand knowledge of these programs—they were not approved for access to nor did they work on these efforts—which likely resulted in misinterpretation of the programs' origins and purpose.

- *The interviewees and others who have mistakenly associated authentic sensitive national security programs with UAP had incomplete or unauthorized access to these programs; discussion of these programs outside of secure facilities presents a high risk of exposing national security information.*

- One named program was a UAP-related Prospective Special Access Program (PSAP) called KONA BLUE that was proposed to the Department of Homeland Security (DHS) and supported by individuals who believed the USG was hiding off-world technology. The program was never approved by DHS and its supporters never provided empirical evidence to support their claims.

- In 2021, without sufficient justification, the scope of an IC Controlled Access Program was expanded to protect UAP reverse-engineering. This program never recovered or reverse-engineered any UAP or extraterrestrial spacecraft. This IC program was disestablished due to its lack of merit.

AARO assesses that the inaccurate claim that the USG is reverse-engineering extraterrestrial technology and is hiding it from Congress is, in large part, the result of circular reporting from a group of individuals who believe this to be the case, despite the lack of any evidence. AARO notes that although claims that the USG has recovered and hidden spacecraft date back to the 1940s and 1950s, more modern instances of these claims largely stem from a consistent group of individuals who have been involved in various UAP-related endeavors since at least 2009.

- Many of these individuals were involved in or supportive of a cancelled DIA program and the subsequent but failed attempt to reestablish this program under DHS, called KONA BLUE.

AARO assesses that UAP sightings and reports of these sightings to USG organizations and claims that some UAP constitute extraterrestrial craft and that the USG has secured and is experimenting on extraterrestrial technology have been influenced by a range of cultural, political, and technological factors. AARO bases this conclusion on the following factors:

9

- The aggregate findings of all USG investigations to date have not found even one case of UAP representing off-world technology.

- None of the programs mentioned by interviewees are UAP reverse-engineering programs, and all the authentic programs have been properly notified and reported to Congress through the congressional defense and/or intelligence committees.

- AARO has no evidence for the USG reverse-engineering narrative provided by interviewees and has been able to disprove the majority of the interviewees' claims. Some claims are still under evaluation.

- AARO determined that a piece of metal alleged to be recovered from an off-world spacecraft is ordinary, of terrestrial origin, and possesses no exceptional qualities.

Several factors—domestic and international—most likely influenced sightings, reports, and the belief by some individuals that there is sufficient proof that some UAP represent extraterrestrial technology. AARO's examination of the historical context of UAP investigations from 1945 to the present reveals that these factors—some common to and distinct between the earlier era of UAP investigations (pre-2009) and the modern era (post-2009)—undoubtedly influenced the direction of these investigations, the volume of and spikes in sightings, and the overall public interest, concern, and debate. These periods are divided into pre- and post-2009 timeframe because this is the year of the standup of the Advanced Aerospace Weapons System Application Program (AAWSAP) and Advanced Aerospace Threat Identification Program (AATIP) efforts. Prior to AAWSAP/AATIP there was about a 40 year gap in UAP investigation programs since the termination of Project BLUE BOOK in 1969.

- Common contextual factors between earlier and modern investigations include a rapidly evolving and dynamic national security environment, concern about technological surprise, intense secrecy related to government military programs, public interest in UAP, perceived bureaucratic barriers, and the persistent lack of quality data.

- Some contextual factors that were distinct between earlier and modern investigations include: differences in the level of public trust in the government; the large volume of popular culture content related to UAP; the perception within some segments of the population that the USG is hiding extraterrestrial technology; unauthorized disclosures of classified programs mistaken for UAP observations; the proliferation of online sources that reinforce these beliefs; the impact that social media has had on circular reporting; and the rapid spread of misinformation.

AARO assesses that some portion of sightings since the 1940s have represented misidentification of never-before-seen experimental and operational space, rocket, and air systems, including stealth technologies and the proliferation of drone platforms. From the 1940s to the 1960s especially, the United States witnessed a boom in experimental technologies driven by World War II and the Cold War.

10

- Many of these technologies fit the description of a stereotypical Unidentified Flying Object (UFO). It is understandable how observers unfamiliar with these programs could mistake sightings of these new technologies as something extraordinary, even other-worldly.

- Along with these conventional technology research areas, the USG started the Manhattan Project in 1942. This program operated in secrecy and led to the establishment of several "secret cities" across the United States to support the development of the nuclear bomb. Any misunderstanding stemming from the intense secrecy surrounding this and similar programs could have been misconstrued for other efforts.

SECTION III: Scope & Assumptions

Scope

This HR2 is provided by DoD in response to a requirement established in the National Defense Authorization Act (NDAA) for FY 2023, Section 6802(j), which states: "Not later than 540 days after the date of the enactment of the Intelligence Authorization Act for Fiscal Year 2023, the Director of the Office shall submit to the congressional defense committees, the congressional intelligence committees and the congressional leadership a written report detailing the historical record of the United States Government relating to unidentified anomalous phenomena." This report, pursuant to the legislation, is based upon the records and documents of the IC and DoD, oral history interviews, open source analysis, interviews of current and former government officials, and classified and unclassified archives.

AARO will provide its findings to Congress in two volumes:

- Volume I contains AARO's findings from 1945 to 31 October 2023 based on the requirements, and:

- Volume II will include any findings resulting from interviews and research completed from 1 November 2023 to 15 April 2024.

AARO interviewed approximately 30 people who claimed to have insight into alleged USG involvement in off-world technology exploitation or to possess knowledge of UAP that have allegedly disrupted U.S. nuclear facilities in the past.

Assumptions

AARO and DoD assume that individuals convey their accurate recollection of their perception of the events they observed or heard. It is important to note that AARO cannot discount nor rely on interviewee accounts alone because of the extraordinary claims contained in their reports. Although individual accounts are important, they are only one element of the larger picture and provide AARO with the opportunity to initiate an investigation. However, any final assessment on the veracity of these accounts must be accompanied by provable facts.

- Some literature suggests individual accounts can be unreliable as they are subject to a person's interpretation of sensory data through the filter of their experiences, beliefs, or state of mind during the event. A person who reports a case might be credible, in that they believe the elements of their account to be accurate. However, their reliability, which is their ability to accurately interpret events—as well as to recall and convey those events due to a range of factors—is altogether different from their inherent sincerity.[1]

- Similarly, confirmation bias is a recognized subconscious cognitive process whereby a person tends to seek and believe information that supports their hypothesis and to discount information that undermines their hypothesis.[2]

- AARO remains open to additional, verifiable information that may alter the conclusions rendered in Volume I and will note any changes to the findings in this report in Volume II.

Note on "UAP" Nomenclature

Use of the UAP naming convention, while imperfect, is the best manner in which to characterize the multitude of unidentified reported sightings. AARO understands that the use of "UAP" to refer to *all* potential possibilities provides a false sense of commonality; such as their origins, identity, purpose, type, and threat they may pose. The only commonality that they all share, at least initially, is that they are each unidentified. Beyond initially being unidentified or misidentified, drones, balloons, aircraft, rockets, rocket exhaust plumes, satellites, infrared (IR) aberrations, sensor artifacts, birds, stars, planets, indistinct lights, vague radar returns, meteors, and optical effects—such as parallax—have nothing in common.

Congressional Oversight

DoD is committed to providing timely and thorough reporting to Congress and to transparency with the American public. Since its establishment, AARO has endeavored to keep Congress fully and currently informed of its activities and findings at all levels of classification. AARO and DoD will continue to share the status and findings of its research at the appropriate level of classification with Congress.

AARO's HR2 Program of Analysis

AARO established six complementary lines of effort (LOEs) to conduct the HR2 research with the goal of ensuring this report conveys an accurate and complete picture. LOEs were conducted in parallel and reinforced each another; a lead in one LOE drove new research and pursuits in another. AARO's goal was to conduct thorough cross-checks to vet all information to discover and close gaps in its understanding. These LOEs were to:

- **Conduct open-source research** on claims (through historical interviews) about USG investigations of, contact with, and recovery of UAP, as well as exploitation of alleged UAP material and technology.

12

- **Conduct classified program research** across the IC, DoD, and interagency to validate or invalidate any claims of classified programs derived from historical interviews.

- **Conduct historical interviews** of individuals who claim knowledge of alleged USG activities related to UAP.

- **Partner with the U.S. National Archives** on locating UAP data, refining requests based on the discovery of new leads derived from historical interviews, as well as open-source and classified research.

- **Engage with commercial entities** on named companies alleged to have worked with the USG on UAP recovery and alleged exploitation of UAP technology.

- **Partner with the archives of key intelligence and national security agencies** such as the Defense Intelligence Agency (DIA), the Central Intelligence Agency (CIA), Department of Energy (DOE), National Security Agency (NSA), the National Geospatial-Intelligence Agency (NGA), the Services, and DoD Combatant Commands.

SECTION IV: Accounts of USG UAP Investigatory Programs Since 1945

Summary

AARO reviewed official USG efforts involving UFOs/UAP since 1945. This research revealed the existence of approximately two dozen separate investigative efforts, depending on how they are counted. These efforts ranged from formal, distinct programs employing a dedicated staff with some measure of longevity including: Projects SAUCER/SIGN, GRUDGE, and BLUE BOOK, the DoD UAP Task Force (UAPTF) led by the U.S. Navy (USN), the Airborne Object Identification and Management Synchronization Group (AOIMSG), and the All-domain Anomaly Resolution Office (AARO). There were also short-term projects that supported some of these established programs including: Projects TWINKLE and BEAR and short-term inquiries into or reviews of specific cases, such as the USAF's two Roswell reports. Additionally, there were efforts that amounted to short-term, outside reviews of USAF-established programs; such as the CIA-sponsored Study Group, the Robertson Panel, the Durant Report, and the University of Colorado's Condon Report (contracted by the USAF). Some of these efforts, including Projects SAUCER and SIGN, were closely connected and essentially the same organization. Project GRUDGE was the name given to two related, but different organizations; the second—reorganized Project GRUDGE—was established about a year after the dissolution of the original Project GRUDGE.

Project SAUCER (1946/1947–January 1948)

Background: The exact date of the founding of this first effort as well as its official and unofficial name are unclear. According to one source, General Nathan Twining, Commander of the Air Technical Services Command, established Project SAUCER on December 30, 1947, to

13

collect and evaluate all information relating to UFO sightings which could be construed as of concern to the national security. Captain Edward Ruppelt claimed that Project SAUCER was the informal name of Project SIGN and it was designated a high priority. However, in an interview with an employee of Project SIGN, the employee claimed the project started a year earlier, in 1946, and that Project SAUCER was its original, informal name. [3] A dearth of data and information is associated with this effort. [4]

Project SAUCER investigated one of the first well-known accounts provided by a private pilot, Kenneth Arnold. The pilot claimed that on June 23, 1947, while flying near Mount Rainier, Washington, he saw nine, large circular objects flying in a formation, objects that periodically flipped and were traveling at 1,700 miles per hour. He also compared the flight characteristics as the "tail of a Chinese kite." [56] Arnold described their shape as "saucer-like aircraft." His account was picked up by several media outlets, and the term "flying saucer" emerged. [7]

Results: Project SAUCER did not find evidence of extraterrestrial technology.

Project SIGN (January 1948–February 1949)

Background: Project SAUCER was formalized into an official, high-priority program named Project SIGN. The Air Technical Intelligence Center (ATIC) assumed control of Project SIGN on January 23, 1948. (ATIC later became the National Air and Space Intelligence Center - NASIC). The impetus for this effort was to determine if these objects might be Soviet secret weapons or "extra-planetary" objects. The staff seemed confident that after a few months of work they could reach a conclusion. As part of their work, the staff at Project SIGN reviewed all of the military's intelligence on German weaponry and aeronautical capabilities to determine if some might have fallen into Soviet possession. [8]

Results: The project evaluated 243 reported UFO sightings, and in February 1949, it concluded that "no definite and conclusive evidence is yet available that would prove or disprove the existence of these unidentified objects as real aircraft of unknown and unconventional configuration." [9] Project SIGN determined that nearly all were caused by either misinterpretation of known objects, hysteria, hallucination, or hoax. [10] It also recommended continued military intelligence control over the investigation of all sightings. It did not rule out the possibility of extraterrestrial phenomena.

- Although the historical account is unsubstantiated and derived from only one source, Project SIGN staff in late July 1948 allegedly drafted, signed, and sent a report ("Estimate of the Situation") up the military chain for approval. This report allegedly concluded that UFOs were "interplanetary" in origin, but it was rejected by USAF Chief of Staff General Hoyt S. Vandenberg as lacking proof. [11]

- This rejected report may have resulted in the Pentagon leadership's loss of confidence in the staff at Project SIGN leading to the establishment of Project GRUDGE, which some sources claim possessed an institutional bias for debunking UFO claims. [12]

Project GRUDGE (Original Organization) (February–December 1949)

Background: Project SIGN was renamed Project GRUDGE in approximately February 1949. The staff, especially those who seemed to lean towards belief in the "interplanetary" origin of UFOs, were reportedly purged from the organization. One account of this time period suggests that because of perceived pressure from the Pentagon's leadership, the remaining staff who held this view changed their minds. This same account claims that the Pentagon's goals for Project GRUDGE were to discount and explain away all reports of UFOs.[13] Project GRUDGE was terminated on December 27, 1949, around the time a comprehensive report on its findings was published. The USAF did not stop collecting and analyzing reports of UFOs; rather, it folded that work into its existing intelligence processes.[14]

Results: Project GRUDGE investigated 244 reports of UFO sightings. It did not discover any evidence that the UAP sightings represented foreign technology; therefore, these findings did not pose a threat to U.S. national security.[15] The report recommended that the organization be downsized and de-emphasized because it was believed Project GRUDGE's very existence fueled a "war hysteria" within the public. The USAF subsequently implemented a public affairs campaign designed to persuade the public that UFOs constituted nothing unusual or extraordinary. The stated goal of this effort was to alleviate public anxiety.[16]

- In August 1949, the USAF asserted that the UFO reports were misinterpretations of natural phenomena, man-made aircraft, fabrications, or hoaxes.[17]

Project TWINKLE (Summer 1949–Summer 1950)

Background: Project TWINKLE was established in the summer of 1949 to investigate a series of UFO reports witnessed by numerous observers in Nevada and New Mexico. These UFOs were described as "green fireballs" streaking across the sky, moving in odd ways, and—in at least one account—the fireball navigated near an aircraft. The literature is not clear if Project TWINKLE was officially supported by the original Project GRUDGE, but it was managed by the USAF's Cambridge Research Laboratory.[18] The goal of this investigation was to use multiple high-powered cameras near White Sands with the hope that if at least two images of the fireballs were captured, then their speed, altitude, and time could be discerned.[19]

Results: This project was only able to secure one camera, which was frequently moved between locations following fireball reports, and no photographs of the fireballs were ever taken.[20]

Project GRUDGE (Reestablishment) (October 1951–March 1952)

Background: In late October 1951, almost two years after Project GRUDGE was disestablished, the USAF's UFO mission was reorganized into another distinct program—also named Project GRUDGE—led by Capt Ruppelt. By his own account, Capt Ruppelt sought to correct the mistakes of Project SIGN and the former Project GRUDGE. His primary goal was to ensure that there would be "no wild speculation" and that if his staff were "too pro or too con" regarding the off-world origin of UFOs, they would be let go. He claimed to have fired three

15

staff. He also realized that he needed a range of scientific expertise which he sourced through a contract he dubbed Project BEAR. Capt Ruppelt set a policy that was intended to foster objectivity. Unlike the previous Project GRUDGE, he allowed his staff to create an "unknown" category of cases which he hoped would dissuade the forcing of a particular answer to any case. The new Project GRUDGE reviewed all of the previous cases in Project SIGN, old Project GRUDGE, and from the ATIC interim period.[21]

Results: The new Project GRUDGE noticed that there was some correlation between sightings and the publication of UFO stories in the media. Capt Ruppelt noted that there were concentrations of cases in the Los Alamos-Albuquerque area, Oak Ridge, White Sands, Strategic Air Command locations, ports, and industrial sites.[22]

- No evidence of extraterrestrial origin of UFO/UAP were discovered.

Project BEAR (Late 1951–Late 1954)

Background: Project BEAR was an informal name given by Capt Ruppelt, Chief of Project GRUDGE, to a contract he created with the Battelle Memorial Institute (BMI) to provide scientific support to the new Project GRUDGE. BMI provided technical support, studied the reliability of interviewee information recall from UFO sightings, created an improved debriefing questionnaire for observers, and developed a computer punch-card system. This system helped automate the statistical study of all the UFO reports in Project GRUDGE's holdings and those in Project BLUE BOOK.[23] BMI released a report under the cover of ATIC to maintain its anonymity. Completed in late 1954, the report was titled "Special Report No. 14."[24]

Results: The Project BEAR report was based on a statistical analysis of UFO sightings and contained graphs showing their frequency and distribution by time, date, location, shape, color, duration, azimuth, and elevation. It concluded that all cases that had enough data were resolved and readily explainable. The report assessed that if more data were available on cases marked unknown, most of those cases could be explained as well. It also concluded that it was highly improbable that any of these cases represented technology beyond their "present day scientific knowledge."[25]

CIA Special Study Group (1952)

Background: After an increase in UFO sightings in 1952, particularly those that gained widespread attention over the Washington, D.C. area during that summer, CIA's Deputy Director for Intelligence, Robert Amory Jr., tasked the CIA Office of Scientific Intelligence's (OSI) Physics and Electronics Division to review UFO cases. A. Ray Gordon took lead on this project, and the Study Group he established reviewed all of ATIC's data (from Projects SIGN through GRUDGE).[26]

Results: The Study Group assessed that 90 percent of the reports were explainable and the other 10 percent amounted to "incredible" claims but rejected the notion that they represented Soviet or extraterrestrial technology. The group also studied Soviet press and found no reports of UFOs, leading the group to assume that the Soviets were deliberately suppressing such reports. The Study Group also believed that the Soviets could use reports of UFOs to create hysteria in the United States or overload the U.S. early-warning system.[27]

- In December 1952, H. Marshall Chadwell, Assistant Director of OSI, briefed the Director of Central Intelligence (DCI), Walter Bedell Smith, on the subject of UFOs. Chadwell urged action because he was convinced that "something was going on that must have immediate attention," and that "sightings of unexplained objects at great altitudes and traveling at high speeds in the vicinity of major U.S. defense installations are of such nature that they are not attributable to natural phenomena or known types of aerial vehicles."[28]

- The source material does not suggest that Smith believed that these sightings were of extraterrestrial origin only that he believed they were not natural phenomena or known competitor technology. It is not clear from the source material why Chadwell seemed to hold a different view than that of the Study Group. It is possible that he suspected that UFO reports represented unknown Soviet technology and therefore posed a national security threat. His concerns about and interest in the topic led to the establishment of the Robertson Panel.

The Robertson Panel (January 1953)

Background: H. Marshall Chadwell clandestinely sponsored the establishment of a UFO scientific review panel led by California Institute of Technology physicist, H.P. Robertson. This action followed a recommendation from CIA's Intelligence Advisory Committee to enlist the services of selected "scientists to review and appraise the available evidence in light of pertinent scientific theories."[29] The panelists had expertise in a range of fields, including nuclear physics, high-energy physics, radar, electronics, and geophysics.[30]

Results: The panel reviewed all USAF data and concluded that most reports had ordinary explanations. The panel unanimously concluded that there was no evidence of a direct threat to U.S. national security from UFOs or that they were of extraterrestrial origin.

- The panel was, however, concerned with the outbreak of mass hysteria and how the Soviets could exploit it. They recommended the USG use various channels to debunk UFO reports and suggested monitoring domestic UFO enthusiast organizations.[31]

- The Robertson Panel discussed the complete lack of the recovery of any "hardware" resulting from "unexplained UFO sightings" which contributed to its assessment that the reported UFOs were neither a foreign threat nor of extraterrestrial origin.[32]

The Durant Report (February 1953)

Background: CIA officer Frederick Durant drafted a report for CIA's Assistant Director of OSI on the Robertson Panel's work and findings. Durant's memorandum provided a brief history of the panel and an unofficial supplement that provided comments and suggestions from members which they had not included in the final report.[33]

17

Results: The report offered no distinct or separate findings of note and mostly summarized the findings of the Robertson Panel.[34]

Project BLUE BOOK (March 1952–December 1969)

Background: USAF Director of Intelligence, Major General Charles P. Cabell, established Project BLUE BOOK to study UFO phenomena. Based at Wright-Patterson Air Force Base near Dayton, Ohio, Project BLUE BOOK was the longest running UFO/UAP investigation. It was led successively by Capt Edward J. Ruppelt (the former Director of the reorganized Project GRUDGE), Capt Charles Hardin, Capt George T. Gregory, Lieutenant Colonel (Lt Col) Roger J. Friend, and Lt Col Hector Quintanilla, Jr. The USAF recorded 12,618 UFO sightings between the years 1947-1969. J. Allen Hynek served as its lead scientific investigator.[35]

Project BLUE BOOK organized its cases into one of three categories: **identified, insufficient data,** and **unidentified.** For those reports that were categorized as identified, Project BLUE BOOK staff used the following categorization schema:

- **Astronomical Sightings**: These consisted of bright stars, planets, comets, fireballs, meteors, auroral streamers, and other celestial bodies. When observed through haze, light fog, moving clouds, or other obscurations or unusual conditions, the planets—including Venus, Jupiter and Mars—were often reported as UFOs.

- **Balloons:** These included weather balloons, radiosondes, and large research balloons with diameters up to 300 feet, which together accounted for several thousand cases. Balloons were released daily from military and civilian airports, weather stations, and research activities. Reflection of the sun on balloons at dawn and sunset sometimes produced strange effects which led to many UFO reports. Large balloons can move at speeds of over 100 miles per hour when in high-altitude wind streams.

- **Aircraft:** According to Project BLUE BOOK, various aircraft accounted for another major source of UFO reports; particularly during adverse weather conditions. The staff noted that when observed at high altitudes and at a distance, the reflection of the sun on aircrafts' surfaces can make them appear as "disc" or "rocket-shaped." They also noted that vapor or condensation trails from jet aircraft will sometimes appear to glow fiery red or orange when reflecting sunlight.

- **Afterburners:** Bright afterburner flames from jet aircraft were often reported as UFOs since they could be seen from great distances when the aircraft was not visible.

- Other UFO resolutions included **stellar mirages, satellites, missiles, reflections, searchlights, birds, kites, false radar indications, fireworks, flares,** and some confirmed **hoaxes**.[36]

Secretary of the Air Force Robert C. Seamans, Jr. announced Project BLUE BOOK's termination on December 17, 1969.[37]

18

AARO partnered with the U.S. National Archives to examine the records from the USAF's Project BLUE BOOK, which spanned from 1947 to 1969. This research presented a significant challenge because of the volume of the documentation amounted to 7,252 files holding a total of 65,778 digital records. The vast majority of the files are populated with USAF documentation. Some cases contain media clippings and images, but these instances are rare.

Results: Project BLUE BOOK determined that:

- No UFO reported, investigated, and evaluated by the USAF demonstrated any indication of a threat to national security.

- There was no evidence submitted to, or discovered by, the USAF that sightings represented technological developments or principles beyond the range of then-present day scientific knowledge.

- There was no evidence indicating that sightings categorized as unidentified are "extraterrestrial vehicles."

- Of the 12,618 sightings in Project BLUE BOOK's holdings, 701 were categorized as unidentified and never solved.[38][39]

CIA Evaluation of UFOs (1964)

Background: Following high-level White House discussions on what to do if alien intelligence was discovered or there was a new outbreak of UFO sightings, DCI John McCone tasked the CIA to update its evaluation of UFOs. The CIA's scientific division officially acquired UFO-sighting case information from the director of the National Investigations Committee on Aerial Phenomena (NICAP), a private organization founded in 1956. [40]

Results: Donald F. Chamberlain, Assistant Director of OSI, subsequently informed McCone that little had changed since the early 1950s; there was still no evidence that UFOs were a threat to the security of the United States or that they were of "foreign origin." [41]

O'Brien Committee (1964)

Background: Dr. Brian O'Brien, a member of the USAF Scientific Advisory Board, chaired the USAF Ad Hoc Review of Project BLUE BOOK. The committee included Carl Sagan, a prominent astronomer from Cornell University.[42]

Results: The committee's report stated that UFOs did not threaten U.S. national security and that it could find no UFO case which represented technological or scientific advances outside of a terrestrial framework. The committee's primary recommendation was that this topic merited intensive academic research and that a top university should lead the study.[43]

The Condon Report (April 1968)

Background: Dr. Edward U. Condon, a physicist and former Director of the National Bureau of Standards, was the scientific director of an 18-month study on "flying saucers" funded under a $325,000 USAF contract to the University of Colorado. This panel took a narrow and somewhat unique view of UFO investigatory efforts, primarily focusing on whether or not UFO phenomena merited formal scientific research in terms of academic or USG-sponsored research and in secondary schools. The panel said their remit did not include the study of UFO phenomena as a potential risk to U.S. national security interests.[44] Among other duties, it closely examined 59 specific case studies.[45]

Results: The panel's report stated that: "Our general conclusion is that nothing has come from the study of UFOs in the past 21 years that has added to scientific knowledge. Careful consideration of the record as it is available to us leads us to conclude that further extensive study of UFOs probably cannot be justified in the expectation that science will be advanced thereby." The panel cautioned against support for scientific papers on this topic and recommended that teachers should not give credit to students for reading UFO literature and materials.[46]

- The panel also investigated and studied a small number of cases of alleged physical evidence of UFO visitations—from imprints on the ground and residue allegedly left behind from UFO landings (such as a white powder and ethereal strands dubbed "angel hair")—to metallic debris. The panel found ordinary explanations for each of these cases. Some of these cases originated in Brazil, Norway, and Washington, D.C.[47]

- The panel investigated a claim made by radio broadcaster Frank Edwards in a 1966 book that a piece of a UFO was recovered near Washington, D.C. in the summer of 1952 during the spike in UFO sightings over the U.S. Capitol in July and August. He claimed that a USN jet fired on a two-foot diameter glowing disc and dislodged a one-pound fragment that was recovered by a ground team. Project BLUE BOOK was not aware of this claim. The USAF and USN found no incident report of weapons engagement with a UFO that summer, no USN aircraft were present, and the retired officer who was the original source of the claim had retired before the summer of 1952, when the event allegedly occurred.[48]

- Edwards also made the claim in 1966 that the USG had loaned the Canadian government fragments of a UFO it had allegedly recovered. It is not clear if this claim was linked to the alleged Washington, D.C. incident. He also claimed that Dr. Vannevar Bush, a prominent inventor, defense industry scientist, and founder of the National Science Foundation, led the effort to study the fragment. The Condon panel determined that these claims most likely were false.[49]

National Academy of Sciences Assessment of the Condon Report (Late 1968)

Background: After the Condon Report was criticized by some scientists—including Project BLUE BOOK's Dr. Hynek—a panel of the National Academy of Sciences (NAS) was tasked in late 1968 to examine the rigor, methodology, and conclusions of the Condon Report. The panel did not conduct its own investigation into the validity of UFO reports.[50]

20

Results: The NAS review concluded that, "We are unanimous in the opinion that this has been a very credible effort to apply...techniques of science to the solution of the UFO problem."[51]

Carter Administration Tasking to National Aeronautics and Space Administration (NASA) (1977)

Background: Dr. Frank Press, Science Advisor to President Jimmy Carter, sent a letter to Dr. Robert Frosch, NASA Administrator, on July 21, 1977, suggesting that a panel be formed by NASA to see if there had been any new significant findings on UFOs since the Condon Report.

Results: Five months later, NASA responded by stating that it was not warranted "to establish a research activity in this area or to convene a symposium on the subject."[52]

Roswell Investigations/Inquiries (1992-2001)

President Clinton and Chief of Staff Podesta Inquire about Roswell (1992 – 2001)
The Roswell Report: Fact versus Fiction in the New Mexico Desert (1995)
The GAO Roswell Report (1995)
The Roswell Report: Case Closed (1997)

Background: According to press reports, President Clinton tasked former National Security Advisor Sandy Berger to determine if the USG held aliens or alien technology. President Clinton said, "As far as I know, an alien spacecraft did not crash in Roswell, New Mexico, in 1947...if the USAF did recover alien bodies, they didn't tell me about it...and I want to know."[53]

In 1993, Congressman Steven H. Schiff (R-New Mexico) made inquiries about the Roswell incident to DoD. The Roswell incident refers to the July 1947 recovery of metallic and rubber debris from a crashed military balloon near Roswell Army Air Field personnel that sparked conspiracy theories and claims that the debris was from an alien spaceship and part of a USG cover-up. He asked the General Accounting Office (GAO) (subsequently renamed the Government Accountability Office) to determine the requirements for reporting air accidents, such as the crash near Roswell, and to identify any government records concerning the Roswell crash.[54]

The USAF conducted a systematic search of numerous archives and records centers in support of GAO's audit of Roswell. As part of this review, the USAF also interviewed numerous people who may have had knowledge of the events. Secretary of the Air Force Sheila E. Widnall released them from any security obligations that may have restricted the sharing of information. The USAF then published *The Roswell Report* in 1995, which included: "The Report of the U.S. Air Force Research Regarding the 'Roswell Incident'" by Col Richard L. Weaver, and the "Synopsis of Balloon Research Findings" by 1st Lt James McAndrew. [55]

Results: The report stated that the USAF's research did not locate or develop any information that indicated the "Roswell Incident" was a UFO event, nor was there any "cover-

21

up" by the USG. Rather, the materials recovered near Roswell were consistent with a balloon of the type used in the then-classified Project Mogul. No records showed any evidence that the USG recovered aliens or extraterrestrial material.[56]

- The USAF subsequently published a follow-on report in 1997, *The Roswell Report: Case Closed*, with additional materials and analysis which supported its conclusion that the debris recovered near Roswell was from the U.S. Army Air Force's balloon-borne program.[57]

- The alleged "alien" bodies reported by some in the New Mexico desert were test dummies that were carried aloft by U.S. Army Air Force high-altitude balloons for scientific research.[58]

- Reports of military units that allegedly recovered a flying saucer and its "crew" were descriptions of Air Force personnel engaged in the dummy recovery operations. Claims of "alien bodies" at the Roswell Army Air Force (RAAF) hospital were most likely the result of the conflation of two separate incidents: a 1956 KC-97 aircraft accident in which 11 Air Force members lost their lives; and a 1959 manned balloon mishap in which two Air Force pilots were injured.[59]

The GAO's 1995 report on the results of its investigation found that that the U.S. Army Air Force regulations in 1947 required that air accident reports be maintained permanently. Four air accidents were reported by the Army Air Force in New Mexico during July 1947. All involved military aircraft and occurred after July 8, 1947—the date the RAAF public information office first reported the crash and recovery of a "flying disc" near Roswell. The military reported no air accidents in New Mexico that month. USAF officials reported to GAO that there was no requirement to prepare a report on the crash of a balloon in 1947.[60]

Advanced Aerospace Weapons System Application Program (AAWSAP) (2009–2012)/ Advanced Aerospace Threat Identification Program (AATIP)

Background: At the direction of Senate Majority Leader Harry Reid (D-NM), the Defense Appropriations Acts of Fiscal Years 2008 and 2010 appropriated $22 million for the DIA to assess long-term and over-the-horizon foreign advanced aerospace threats to the United States. In coordination with the Office of the Under Secretary of Defense for Intelligence, DIA established AAWSAP in 2009, which was also known AATIP. The contract for this DIA-managed program was awarded to a private sector organization.[61] *[Note on program names: The names AAWSAP and AATIP have been used interchangeably for the name of this program, including on official documentation. Unlike AAWSAP, AATIP was never an official DoD program. However, after AAWSAP was cancelled, the AATIP moniker was used by some individuals associated with an informal, unofficial UAP community of interest within DoD that researched UAP sightings from military observers as part of their ancillary job duties. This effort was not a recognized, official program, and had no dedicated personnel or budget.]*

- The primary purpose of AAWSAP/AATIP was to investigate potential next generation aerospace technologies in 12 specific areas—such as advanced lift,

22

propulsion, the use of unconventional materials and controls, and signature reduction.[62]

- Although investigating UFO/UAP was not specifically outlined in the contract's statement of work, the selected private sector organization conducted UFO research with the support of the DIA program manager. This research included: reviewing new cases and much older Project BLUE BOOK cases, operating debriefing and investigatory teams, and proposals to set up laboratories to examine any recovered UFO materials.[63]

- AAWSAP/AATIP also investigated an alleged hotspot of UAP and paranormal activity at a property in Utah—which at that time was owned by the head of the private sector organization—including examining reports of "shadow figures" and "creatures," and exploring "remote viewing" and "human consciousness anomalies." The organization also planned to hire psychics to study "inter-dimensional phenomena" believed to frequently appear at that location.[64]

- DIA did not seek, nor specifically authorize, this work though a DIA employee set up and managed the contract with the private sector organization.[65]

- On 24 June 2009, Senator Reid sent a letter to then Deputy Secretary of Defense William Lynn III requesting that AAWSAP/AATIP be made a DoD Special Access Program. Deputy Secretary Lynn declined to do so based on the recommendation of then-Under Secretary of Defense for Intelligence, James R. Clapper, Jr., that such a designation was not justified.[66]

- Just prior to DoD's cancellation of the program, the private sector organization proposed as a new line of effort to host a series of "intellectual debates" at academic institutes to influence the public debate, which included hiring supportive reporters and celebrity moderators. The goal of this proposed public relations campaign was to assume that "E.T. visitations are true" and that the moderators would steer debate away from "dead-end discussions" and the "morass" about discussing "evidence."[67] A stated goal of this proposal was to increase public interest in government "disclosure" around the "E.T. topic" and explore the consequences of disclosure on the public.[68]

Results: The AAWSAP/AATIP contract with the private sector organization produced exploratory papers addressing the 12 scientific areas tasked in the contract's statement of work. These scientific papers were never thoroughly peer reviewed.

- AARO has yet to uncover any other substantive UAP case work conducted by AAWSAP/AATIP. Instead, AAWSAP/AATIP reviewed a large number of Project BLUE BOOK and private cases and conducted interviews of UAP observers and conducted unrelated work on alleged paranormal activities at the private sector organization's property in Utah.

- AAWSAP/AATIP was terminated in 2012 upon the completion of its deliverables due to DIA and DoD concerns about the project.

23

- After AAWSAP/AATIP was terminated, its supporters unsuccessfully attempted to convince DHS to support a new version of this effort dubbed KONA BLUE.

Unidentified Aerial Phenomena Task Force (UAPTF) (August 2020-November 2021)

Background: Deputy Secretary of Defense David L. Norquist approved the establishment of the UAPTF in August 2020. Under the cognizance of the Office of the Under Secretary of Defense for Intelligence and Security (USD(I&S)), the Department of the Navy was asked to lead the task force. It was established to improve understanding of, and gain insight into, the nature and origins of UAP. The task force's mission was to detect, analyze, and catalog UAP that could potentially pose a threat to U.S. national security.[69]

Results: The UAPTF helped standardize, destigmatize, and increase the volume of UAP reporting. Its work also helped calibrate sensors to improve the quality of data collected. Its methods and processes directly led to the identification of the People's Republic of China's (PRC) high altitude balloons that traversed over the continental United States.[70]

Preliminary Assessment: Unidentified Aerial Phenomena (June 2021)

Background: Senate Report 116-233, accompanying the Intelligence Authorization Act for Fiscal Year 2021, directed the Office of the Director of National Intelligence (ODNI) in consultation with the Secretary of Defense to submit an intelligence assessment of the threat posed by UAP and to report on the progress the UAPTF had made in understanding this threat.

Results: The preliminary assessment concluded that: (1) the limited amount of high-quality reporting on UAP hampers the ability to draw firm conclusions about their nature or intent; (2) in a limited number of incidents, UAP reportedly appeared to exhibit unusual flight characteristics; although those observations could be the result of sensor errors, spoofing, or observer misperception and require additional rigorous analysis; (3) there are probably multiple types of UAP requiring different explanations based on the range of appearances and behaviors described in the available reporting; (4) UAP may pose airspace safety issues and a challenge to U.S. national security; and (5) consistent consolidation of reports from across the USG, standardized reporting, increased collection and analysis, and a streamlined process for screening all such reports against a broad range of relevant government data will allow for a more sophisticated analysis of UAP.[71]

Airborne Object Identification and Management Synchronization Group (AOIMSG) / Airborne Object Identification and Management Executive Management Committee (AOIMEXEC) (November 2021-June 2022)

Background: The Deputy Secretary of Defense, in consultation with the Director of National Intelligence (DNI), directed USD(I&S) to establish AOIMSG to succeed the USN's UAPTF.[72]

Results: The organization helped initiate synchronization of efforts across the Department and the broader USG to detect, identify, and attribute objects of interests in "Special Use Airspace," as well as to assess and mitigate any associated threats to safety of flight and national security.[73] AOIMSG had not achieved initial operating capability before subsequent legislation in the FY2022 NDAA resulted in it being renamed to AARO and given an expanded mission set.

UAP Independent Study Team (UAPIST) (June 2022-September 2023)

Background: NASA established the UAPIST as a subordinate group of its Earth Science Advisory Committee, which was established in accordance with the Federal Advisory Committee Act. The UAPIST examined UAP from a scientific perspective, focusing on how NASA can use data and the scientific tools to achieve a better understanding of UAP. The Assistant Deputy Associate Administrator for Research at NASA's Science Mission Directorate was responsible for orchestrating the study. The independent study team was chaired by the President of the Simons Foundation and included members from the USG, academia, and the private sector.[74]

Results: NASA released its report in September 2023. The report focused on discovering the best data streams available and discoverable to resolve UAP cases. It did not focus on whether or not UAP were of extraterrestrial origin. NASA also established a UAP Research Director position.

All-domain Anomaly Resolution Office (AARO) (Established July 15, 2022)

Background: In response to the NDAA for FY22, the Deputy Secretary of Defense in coordination with the DNI, conveyed direction to the USD(I&S) by renaming the AOIMSG as AARO, and expanded its scope and mission.[75] AARO organized itself around four functions (analysis, operations, science & technology (S&T), and strategic communications). AARO is developing IC and S&T analytic tradecraft practices, implementing a science testing plan, implementing a secure interviewee debriefing program, and is working to standardize UAP collection and reporting across the DoD and the IC.

Results: Consistent with congressional direction, AARO provides quarterly reports, semiannual briefings, and an annual report to Congress in coordination with the ODNI. In addition, on January 12, 2023, the ODNI submitted the 2022 Annual Report on Unidentified Aerial Phenomena to Congress. This report was drafted in partnership with AARO and based on AARO's data.

- The report stated that there was a total of 510 UAP reports as of August 30, 2022. This included the 144 UAP reports covered during the 17 years of reporting included in the ODNI's preliminary assessment, as well as 247 new reports and 119 reports that subsequently were discovered or reported.

- The report also stated that UAP events continue to occur in restricted or sensitive airspace, highlighting possible concerns for safety of flight or adversary collection activity.[76]

25

- The AARO Director reported to Congress that the majority of cases in AARO's holdings have ordinary explanation and that AARO has not seen any evidence that any of these cases represent extraterrestrial technology.

- ***Of all the reports that AARO investigated and analyzed, none represent extraterrestrial or off-world technology. A small percentage of cases have potentially anomalous characteristics or concerning characteristics. AARO has kept Congress fully and currently informed of its findings. AARO's research continues on these cases.***

Foreign and Academic Investigatory Efforts

AARO reviewed seven other UAP investigatory panels and programs sponsored by a U.S. university, the United Kingdom, Canada, and France. Of these efforts, one unofficial report from a Canadian government effort in the early 1950s claimed UFOs were of extraterrestrial origin, and the program director claimed he was in contact with aliens. This position appeared to reflect the opinions of the director of the effort and was not endorsed or supported by the Canadian government.

- Stanford University's **Sturrock Panel** (1998) found no convincing evidence for the extraterrestrial origin of UFO/UAP.[77]

- The United Kingdom's **Flying Saucer Working Party** (1950–1951) concluded that "flying saucers did not exist."[78]

- Canada's **Sky Project** (2023) is currently ongoing, and the program will release its findings in 2024.[79]

- Canada's **Project Second Storey** (1952-1954), an advisory committee that advised the government, never reached any significant conclusions.[80]

- Canada's **Project Magnet** (1950-1954) was run by Department of Transport engineer Wilbert B. Smith. Smith assessed that UFOs were of extraterrestrial origin and that they flew by magnetism. Smith believed he was in personal contact with extraterrestrial beings through telepathy and "tensor beams." Smith, in an interview as early as 1961, claimed that in 1952, the USAF lent him a piece of a UFO to study. He also claimed it was composed of magnesium orthosilicate. The Canadian government closed the project, saying that there were no definitive results from the research. Smith admitted that his beliefs concerning UFOs were his alone and not the government's official position.[81]

- The French government sponsored three comprehensive investigatory programs: Groupe d'Etude et d'Information sur les Phénomènes Aérospatiaux Non-identifiés (GEPAN, 1977-1987), Service d'Expertise des Phénomènes de Rentrées Atmosphériques (SEPRA, 1988-2004), and a new version called Groupe d'Etudes et d'Informations sur les Phénomènes Aérospatiaux Non-identifiés (GEIPAN) that stood up in 2005. When it dissolved, SERPA concluded that the vast majority of cases

26

possess ordinary explanations, while 28 percent of its caseload remained unresolved. None of these organizations have found evidence of extraterrestrial visitations to Earth.[82]

Key Findings

- None of these investigations (including USG, foreign, and U.S. academic efforts) reached the conclusion that any of the UAP reports indicated extraterrestrial origin.

- All of these efforts and reviews concluded that the vast majority of UAP reports could be resolved as any number of ordinary objects, natural phenomena, optical illusions or misidentifications. Many of the cases, however, remain unresolved.

- The lack of actionable, researchable data—specifically the lack of speed, altitude, and size of reported UAP—combined with resource constraints, high volumes of cases, and perceived differing levels of support from USG officials were factors in all investigative efforts. Even with the significant advancements in ground- and air-based sensors, the apparent inability to collect sufficient and high-quality data for scientific analysis continues to plague investigations.

- Three efforts investigated reports of direct or indirect physical evidence of UFOs (from depressions on the ground to metallic debris) and found nothing of foreign or extraterrestrial origin.

- There was at least one USG proposal—by the CIA-sponsored Robertson Panel—to engage in an active "training" and "debunking" effort using various public media tools to steer the public away from reporting UFOs. The proposal reasoned that it did not believe UFOs were foreign technological threats or of extraterrestrial origin; rather, it viewed the persistent flood of reports as cluttering and bogging down government processes, expressing the concern that such reports could create "mass hysteria" to the benefit of the Soviet Union.

- At various points in history, individuals inside and outside of the USG, including Dr. J. Allen Hynek, claimed the USAF had a key goal of debunking or explaining away reports of UAP. AARO found no evidence to suggest that the USAF had a policy intended to cover up the evidence of extraterrestrial knowledge, material, or interactions. Rather, the USAF instead sought to focus on what it determined to be more important concerns, such as Soviet technology and U.S. defense readiness. Similarly, at least the first iteration of Project GRUDGE sought to resolve all cases and prohibited its staff from characterizing reports as unknown or unidentified.

- AARO notes that there was possibly one *unofficial* estimate stating otherwise. Project SIGN staff allegedly drafted and signed a report that was circulated for review and approval. It was titled: "The Estimate of the Situation" and assessed that at least some UFOs were of "interplanetary" origin. The DoD leadership rejected this report on the basis that it lacked any proof, and it was never published. The first Director of

27

Project BLUE BOOK, Capt Edward Ruppelt, said that all but a couple copies of this estimate were destroyed. [83] AARO has been unable to verify his claim or locate the document.

SECTION V: Assessment of Interviewee Claims of USG Involvement in Hidden UAP Programs

Summary

As of September 17, 2023, AARO interviewed approximately 30 individuals. AARO categorized these individuals into three tiers: Tier 1 interviewees are those who have spoken with congressional staff or Members of Congress and have been subsequently referred to AARO; Tier 2 interviewees are those who have been referred to AARO by Tier 1 interviewees; Tier 3 interviewees are AARO-generated interviewees that have a corroborating touchpoint to the principal integrated narrative of reports from Tier 1 and Tier 2 interviewees. Priority is given to those interviewees who claimed firsthand knowledge of government programs, events, or details about any resulting material. Interviewees relaying second or thirdhand knowledge are lower in priority, but AARO has and will continue to schedule interviews with them, nonetheless.

AARO generated random numbers and assigned one to each interviewee. AARO maintains the key, which is stored and handled in a secure manner to protect each interviewee's privacy. In some instances, AARO assigned a random number to a person who has not interviewed with AARO but was referenced by interviewees as a key individual. AARO also assigned numbers to organizations mentioned by interviewees.

AARO assesses that two main narratives have emerged, with various and potentially unrelated offshoots:

Primary Narrative

The primary narrative alleges that *the USG and industry partners are in possession of and are testing off-world technology that has been concealed from congressional oversight and the world since approximately 1964, and possibly since 1947, if the Roswell events are included.* The narrative asserts that this UAP program possesses as many as 12 extraterrestrial spacecraft.

- An AARO interviewee[84] claimed in a thirdhand account that an organization[85] was in possession of 12 spacecraft recovered from different crash events prior to 1970. Some of the craft allegedly were "intact." The interviewee also stated that the CIA had a partnership with the company that ended in 1989 and wanted all material returned to the CIA. AARO discovered no empirical evidence supporting these claims.

- An interviewee[86] claimed that an organization[87] was in possession of off-world material in 2009 and 2010. A separate interviewee stated they participated in negotiations to return the material to the USG. The same interviewee stated that a

28

former named senior CIA official quashed the proposal to remove the material from the corporation.

- A separate interviewee[88] claimed that circa 1999, a former, senior U.S. military officer[89] told the interviewee that that he touched the surface of an extraterrestrial spacecraft. The interviewee stated that the senior officer gave a detailed description of a craft floating in a building. The officer told the interviewee that approximately 150 individuals were working on the program and that the program was kept "outside of government" so the technology could remain proprietary.

- Two interviewees[90] said they participated in an alleged White House-tasked UAP study in Northern Virginia sometime between 2004 and 2007. The study evaluated the impacts to society should the United States, Russia, or China disclose they had evidence of extraterrestrial beings or craft. One interviewee assumed these governments possessed such evidence.[91] The study was conducted by approximately 12 participants who evaluated 64 different aspects of society, such as religion and financial markets, which could be impacted by such a disclosure.[92] The study lasted one day, and the interviewee was not aware of any final report or to whom any report may have been delivered.

- Another interviewee claimed that in the 1990s he overhead electronic communication of a conversation between two military bases where scientists claimed "aliens" were present during specialized materials testing.[93] The interviewee also reported that on another occasion in the 1990s he observed an "unidentified flying object" at a U.S. military facility. The interviewee described the object as exhibiting a peculiar flight pattern.

- An interviewee who is a former U.S. service member said that in 2009, while participating in a humanitarian and security mission in a foreign country, he encountered "U.S. Special Forces" loading containers onto a large extraterrestrial spacecraft. [94]

- A separate interviewee said that a family member was part of an effort to reverse-engineer an object assumed to be off-world technology in the 1980s.[95] The engineers failed to reverse-engineer the object and it was sent to a different facility for further evaluation.

- An interviewee pointed out to AARO the existence of an alleged leaked Special National Intelligence Estimate from 1961 as proof of the existence of UAP crashes.[96] AARO obtained a copy of the document through open-source research and evaluated its authenticity.

- Some interviewees and public accounts underpin this storyline by claiming through second and thirdhand accounts that some NDAs may have been used to protect a "reverse-engineering program of off-world technology." These accounts describe the NDAs as including "punishment by death" provisions should the signatory disclose

29

information about the program. Some interviewees claimed "verbal" and written NDAs were administered in several instances.[97]

Secondary Narrative

The other narrative is that *a cluster of UAP sightings that occurred in close proximity to U.S. nuclear facilities have resulted in the malfunctioning and destruction of nuclear missiles and a test reentry vehicle.* AARO interviewed five former USAF members who served in and around U.S. intercontinental ballistic missile (ICBM) silos at Malmstrom, Ellsworth, Vandenberg, and Minot USAF bases between 1966 and 1977.[98] Some of these individuals claim UAP sightings near the silos, while others claim UAP disruptions to ICBM operations. Specifically, they said the ICBM launch control facilities went offline or experienced total power failure. Additionally, one interviewee and a USAF videographer claimed to have observed and recorded a UAP destroying an ICBM loaded with a "dummy" warhead, mid-flight. AARO is researching U.S. and adversarial activity related to these events, including any U.S. programs that tested defensive ballistic missile capabilities.

Findings

AARO investigated and reached conclusions on the majority of the claims made in these narratives. In most cases, AARO was able to locate the companies, people, and programs that were conveyed to AARO through interviews. AARO will report the results of the unresolved allegations in Volume II. AARO's findings to date are as follows:

No Official UAP Nondisclosure Agreements Discovered

In the conduct of this review, and to meet the direction of Section 1673 of the NDAA for FY 2023, AARO sent guidance and requests to DoD, IC elements, DOE, and DHS to review and provide any NDAs pertaining to UAP (or its previous names). To date, AARO personnel have not discovered or been notified of any NDAs that contain information related to UAP. Also, apart from the standard NDA language contained in Title 18, Section 794 describing the death penalty or jail time for illegally disclosing information relating to the national defense, AARO has not discovered any NDAs containing threats to interviewees for disclosing UAP-specific information.

Historically, most if not all NDAs contained standard language stating that the death penalty can be applied for the crime of disclosing classified information. Title 18, Section 794, is referenced in typical NDAs in several places in relation to the transmission of classified information:

> *"Whoever, with intent or reason to believe that it is to be used to the injury of the United States or to the advantage of a foreign nation, communicates, delivers, or transmits…information relating to the national defense, **shall be punished by death** or by imprisonment for any term of years or for life…."*

Former CIA Official Involvement in Movement of Alleged Material Recovered from a UAP Crash Denied on the Record

AARO interviewed and obtained a signed statement from the former CIA official who was specifically named by AARO interviewees. The former official stated he had no knowledge of any aspect of this allegation.[99] The allegation included the claimed crash of the objects, the possession of the resultant material by the USG and the private sector, and the attempt to transfer material that was purported to be of off-world origin. This reverse-engineering program allegedly occurred at the named facility in the 2009-2010 time frame. Interviewees allege that a separate interviewee[100] from the facility attempted to set up a meeting to return material to the USG in 2010, but that the former CIA official stopped the transfer from industry to the USG. The interviewee alleged to have stopped the transfer denied these allegations.[101] The former CIA official stated that he had no knowledge of any extraterrestrial material in the possession of the USG or any other organization.[102] The official signed a Memorandum for the Record (MFR) attesting to the truthfulness of his statements.

The 1961 Special National Intelligence Estimate on "UFOs" Assessed to be Not Authentic

An interviewee [103] brought to AARO's attention the existence of an alleged Special National Intelligence Estimate (SNIE), dated November 5, 1961, titled: "Critical Aspects of Unidentified Flying Objects and the Nuclear Threat to the Defense of the United States and its Allies." Through open-source research, AARO obtained a copy of the document. After discussions with the CIA's Center for the Study of Intelligence (CSI), the NSA Scientific Studies Board (one of the alleged authors), and research comparing this document to a number of known SNIEs and National Intelligence Estimates, AARO concluded the document is not authentic. NSA archives were searched because "the NSA Scientific Advisory Board" purportedly was one of the document's authors. CIA/CSI and NSA did not possess nor have knowledge of the document. AARO found the document lacked IC tradecraft standards and possessed significant inconsistencies with SNIE's and National Intelligence Estimates of the general time period. These inconsistencies included: the document's short length, incorrect formatting, inconsistent branding, lack of a dissemination block and coordination language, loose narrative style, convoluted logic, imprecise and casual language, and its superficial treatment of globally significant issues.

Aliens Observing Material Test a Likely Misunderstanding of an Authentic, Non-UAP Program Activity

AARO determined this account most likely amounted to a misunderstanding. The conversation likely referenced a test and evaluation unit that had a nickname with "alien" connotations at the specific installation mentioned. The nature of the test described by the interviewee[104] closely matched the description of a specific materials test conveyed to AARO investigators.

31

Allegation that a Former U.S. military Service Member Touched an Extraterrestrial Spacecraft

An interviewee[105] stated that a former military member, who was also an interviewee, had stated that he had touched an off-world aircraft. AARO contacted and interviewed the former military member[106] who denied any knowledge of off-world technology in possession of the USG, a private contractor, or any other foreign or domestic entity. The former military member attested that he could not remember if this encounter with the original interviewee had ever occurred, but opined that if it had happened, the only situation that he might have conveyed was the time when he touched an F-117 Nighthawk stealth fighter at a facility. The former military member signed an MFR attesting to the truthfulness of his account.

The UAP with Peculiar Characteristics Refers to an Authentic, Non-UAP-Related SAP

AARO was able to correlate this account with an authentic USG program because the interviewee was able to provide a relatively precise time and location of the sighting which they observed exhibiting strange characteristics. At the time the interviewee said he observed the event, DoD was conducting tests of a platform protected by a SAP. The seemingly strange characteristics reported by the interviewee match closely with the platform's characteristics, which was being tested at a military facility in the time frame the interviewee was there. This program is not related in any way to the exploitation of off-world technology.

Extraterrestrial Disclosure Study Confirmed; Not White House-Sponsored

An organization[107] in Northern Virginia did conduct a study between 2004 and 2007 on the societal effects should the United States or other world governments disclose they have evidence of extraterrestrial life. Interviewees believed the White House sponsored it. AARO confirmed through two former White House senior officials[108] that the White House did not request it, nor were they aware of any such study.

Aerospace Companies Denied Involvement in Recovering Extraterrestrial Craft

AARO met with high-ranking officials, including executives and chief technology officers, of the named companies. All denied the existence of these programs, and attested to the truthfulness of their statements on the record.

Sample of Alleged Alien Spacecraft is an Ordinary, Terrestrial, Metal Alloy

AARO learned through an interviewee that a private sector organization[109] claimed to have in its possession material from an extraterrestrial craft recovered from a crash at an unknown location from the 1940s or 1950s. The organization claimed that the material had the potential to act as a THz frequency waveguide, and therefore, could exhibit "anti-gravity" and "mass reduction" properties under the appropriate conditions. The organization that owned the material negotiated an agreement in 2019 with the U.S. Army to analyze the samples. With permission from the stakeholders, AARO acquired this sample to conduct more in-depth analyses.

- *AARO and a leading science laboratory concluded that the material is a metallic alloy, terrestrial in nature, and possibly of USAF origin, based on its materials characterization.* It was also assessed that the material is mostly composed of magnesium, and the bismuth present was not a pure layer per initial claims.

- The U.S. Army had also conducted in-house analysis on the sample, and while AARO generally agrees with its conclusions, AARO found that the structure was not purely layered magnesium alloy and bismuth.

AARO assesses that a separate private sector organization's recreation of this metallic sample was almost certainly conflated with claims that the aerospace industry was attempting to reverse-engineer off-world technology. Prior to AARO's acquisition of the sample, the organization fabricated a replica of the sample to determine if it could be done.[110]

- *The same organization[111] made an attempt to replicate the sample at the same specific location cited by the interviewee[112] as the location where the interviewee alleged to have participated in discussions about transferring UAP crash materials.* The claim that extraterrestrial technology was being reverse-engineered almost certainly was conflated with this material fabrication.

AARO Investigating Unresolved Historical Nuclear-Related UAP Cases

Like all historical UAP cases, very little actionable data exists beyond limited firsthand narrative accounts. Nevertheless, AARO continues to investigate these cases due to the sensitive nature of these events potentially impacting the readiness of the U.S. nuclear program. Although AARO has not been able to recover the alleged film of the ballistic missile reentry vehicle being shot down by a UAP in 1964, AARO was able to correlate the general time and location with an antiballistic missile test, which could have been the genesis for this observation.

SECTION VI: Investigation into Named USG Sensitive Programs

Summary

AARO investigated numerous named, and described, but unnamed programs alleged to involve UAP exploitation conveyed to AARO through official interviews. Although at least one interviewee claimed to have seen a captured UAP, none of the interviewees had direct access to or firsthand knowledge of the programs alleged to be UAP-related. One interviewee had access into one authentic program, but his position was such that he had only limited access to its complete details. Interviewees' indirect and incomplete knowledge of authentic efforts most likely contributed to their misinterpretation of what they heard or saw.

- *AARO concludes many of these programs represent authentic, current and former sensitive, national security programs, but none of these programs have been involved with capturing, recovering, or reverse-engineering off-world technology or material.*

33

- All the programs assessed to be authentic were or—if still active—continue to be, appropriately reported to either or both the congressional defense and intelligence committees.

Process for Protecting Sensitive Programs while Investigating Interviewee Claims

AARO instituted a secure process for handling information to allow interviewees to come forward to provide their statements to AARO within secure facilities. AARO established a partnership with the Special Access Program Control Offices for the DoD, IC, and DHS to review programs identified in interviews by name or description to determine if the programs correlated in time and location to historic SAP or Controlled Access Programs (CAP). This agreement details how interviewee claims concerning the names and descriptions of the alleged programs are handled, stored, and protected so that their veracity can be determined in a secure manner. A key part of this agreement is that AARO investigators have been granted full access to all pertinent sensitive USG programs.

- When industry partners were named, AARO interviewed senior level, appropriately-cleared executives, department leads, senior scientists, and engineers.

Findings

One Private Program Mistaken for USG Program

AARO determined that the following alleged USG program name was portrayed inaccurately by the interviewee:

- Virtual Institute for Satellite Integration Training–This program is not a USG-funded and supported effort. It was a program operated by a private UAP organization and had a NASA engineer as a participant. NASA verified that it did not sponsor the project.[113]

KONA BLUE: A Proposed UAP Recovery and Reverse-Engineering Program

KONA BLUE was brought to AARO's attention by interviewees who claimed that it was a sensitive DHS compartment to cover up the retrieval and exploitation of "non-human biologics."[114] KONA BLUE traces its origins to the DIA-managed AAWSAP/AATIP program, which was funded through a special appropriation and executed by its primary contractor, a private sector organization. DIA cancelled the program in 2012 due to lack of merit and the utility of the deliverables. As discussed in Section IV of this report, while the official purpose of AAWSAP/AATIP was to conduct research into 12 areas of cutting edge science, the contractor team, and at least one supportive government program manager, also conducted UAP and paranormal research at a property owned by the private sector organization.

When DIA cancelled this program, its supporters proposed to DHS that they create and fund a new version of AAWSAP/AATIP under a SAP.[115] This proposal, codenamed KONA BLUE, would restart UAP investigations, paranormal research (including alleged "human consciousness anomalies") and reverse-engineer any recovered off-world spacecraft that they hoped to acquire. This proposal gained some initial traction at DHS to the point where a

34

Prospective Special Access Program (PSAP) was officially requested to stand up this program, but it was eventually rejected by DHS leadership for lacking merit. As demonstrated by the proposal package and by statements from the originator, Senators Lieberman and Reid asked that the PSAP be established with the promise of additional funding.[116] The proposed KONA BLUE lines of effort closely mirrored those conducted by the private sector organization for AAWSAP/AATIP.

KONA BLUE's advocates were convinced that the USG was hiding UAP technologies. They believed that creating this program under DHS would allow all of the technology and knowledge of these alleged programs to be moved under the KONA BLUE program. The program would provide a security and governing structure where it could be monitored properly by congressional oversight committees. This belief was foundational for the KONA BLUE proposal, based on the proposal documents and several interviewees who have provided the same information to AARO and Congress.[117] The *Oral History Initiative* section of the KONA BLUE proposal was to collect data:

> "…from an already identified and calibrated list of retired, previously highly placed government, armed services, contractor and intelligence community individuals. The oral history project will include gathering all information pertaining to the location of advanced aerospace technology and biological samples, including records, files, reports, photographs, as well as physical samples."[118]

It is critical to note that no extraterrestrial craft or bodies were ever collected—this material was only assumed to exist by KONA BLUE advocates and its anticipated contract performers. This was the same assumption made by those same individuals involved with the AAWSAP/AATIP program. The SAP was never approved or stood up, and no data or material was transferred to DHS.[119]

- KONA BLUE was not reported to Congress at that time because it was never established as a SAP and, therefore, did not meet the threshold for congressional reporting. However, the Deputy Secretary of Defense provided a Congressional Notification concerning the program when it was identified in the spirit of transparency.

Unnecessary IC Program Expansion

AARO confirmed the existence of one IC CAP that was unnecessarily expanded in 2021 to include a UAP reverse-engineering mission. This program was expanded despite the lack of any evidence or mission need to justify the expansion. The appropriate congressional committees were notified. This program never recovered or reverse-engineered any technology, let alone off-world spacecraft. This CAP was disestablished due to its inactivity, absence of mission need, and lack of merit.

Nexus of Proponents of the USG UAP Reverse-Engineering Allegation

AARO found no empirical evidence that any UAP investigatory effort since 1945— foreign, domestic, government, private, or academic—has ever uncovered verifiable information regarding the recovery or existence of extraterrestrial beings or crafts. Although AARO continues to conduct interviews, research programs, and pursue investigatory leads, AARO's work has resulted in disproving the majority of these claims using the verifiable information made within those claims.

AARO researched and interviewed numerous people, programs, and leads. It has determined that modern allegations that the USG is hiding off-world technology and beings largely originate from the same group of individuals who have ties to the cancelled AAWSAP/AATIP program and a private sector organization's paranormal research efforts. These individuals have worked with each other consistently in various UAP-related efforts.

- Persons 1-5 and Interviewees 1, 3, 9, 12, 13, and 14 have repeatedly voiced these claims in various public and private venues, and they have petitioned Congress in various capacities on UAP issues. They have not provided any empirical evidence of their claims to AARO. [120]

- Persons 1 and 3 and Interviewees 1, 3, and 12 were involved with the paranormal research conducted under AAWSAP/AATIP. [121]

- Person 5 and Interviewees 3, 9 and 14 were involved with the alleged crashed UAP materials that were provided to the U.S. Army and subsequently to AARO for examination. [122]

- Persons 4, 7, and 8 and Interviewees 1, 3, and 13 investigated UAP on their own and were responsible for successfully expanding the remit of an existing IC program to include UAP exploitation language. [123]

- AARO notes that Persons 1 and 4 never formally sat down with AARO to provide official, signed statements; these individuals have been mentioned by other interviewees frequently as sources of their claims. Person 8 held an informal interview and Interviewee 14 sat for an official interview but has not signed the memo for the record documenting this interview.

SECTION VII: Historical Context of UAP Investigatory Efforts Since 1945

Summary

AARO assesses that the incidents of UAP sightings reported to USG organizations, the claims that some constitute extraterrestrial craft, and the claims that the USG has secured and is experimenting on alien technology, most likely are the result of a range of cultural, political, and technological factors. AARO bases this conclusion on the aggregate findings of all USG investigations to date, the misinterpretation of all reported named sensitive programs, the lack of empirical evidence to support the USG reverse-engineering narrative, and AARO's assessment that the piece of metal alleged to be recovered from an alien spacecraft in the late 1940s is ordinary, of terrestrial origin, and possesses no exceptional qualities.

- Although many cases remain unsolved—primarily because of the lack of actionable and researchable data—AARO and its predecessor organizations concluded that the

36

vast majority of cases report on events that amount to ordinary objects, atmospheric and natural phenomena, and observer misidentification.

- Although many UAP/UFO cases remain unsolved, based on the lack of evidence of the extraterrestrial origin of even one UAP report and the assessment that all resolved cases to date have ordinary explanations, AARO assess sightings and claims of extraterrestrial visitations have been influenced by a range of factors.

Commonalities of 20th and 21st Century UAP Investigations

International Security Environment and Technological Surprise

In both periods, changes in the international order brought uncertainty. Concern about the Soviet Union's desire for regional hegemony and military and political superiority contributed to U.S. involvement with conflicts in Korea, Vietnam, and elsewhere, sparked a boom in U.S. technological innovation, and led to widespread fear within society about Soviet capabilities and intentions.

One primary means of competing with the Soviet Union was to collect intelligence on Soviet leadership intentions and military capabilities. The means by which the U.S. accomplished this goal was to develop a range of air- and space-based reconnaissance systems to collect an array of intelligence on the Soviet Union—especially over its territory. During some early UFO investigation efforts, it was deemed essential to determine if UFOs were Soviet "secret weapons" or psychological warfare operations aimed at causing public fear and generating hysteria to undermine U.S. societal morale.

Today's global security environment is similarly dynamic. Both the Russian Federation and the PRC seek to alter the international system at the expense of the security of the United States. AARO recognizes that concern with competitor technological surprise is still a real and legitimate driver of UAP investigations today. It is imperative to determine whether or not these sightings represent a risk to flight safety, and whether these sightings represent technological advances that could pose counterintelligence and national security threats.

Secrecy

The USG's need to maintain secrecy to protect classified information about intelligence sources and methods, military operations and technology, and U.S. vulnerabilities is also a shared context among all UAP investigations. While secrecy is essential to protect U.S. national security interests, it can reduce the public's trust in government. With a gap in information about UFO/UAP investigations, other information sources and narratives, including private UFO investigative organizations and "UFOlogy" emerged to fill that gap. AARO assesses that the classification of prior USG investigations have fueled speculation that the government was hiding knowledge of extraterrestrials, when, in fact, secrecy was and still is intended to deliberately and thoughtfully protect sensitive military and intelligence community programs, capabilities, sources, and methods.

Public Interest

Segments of the American public have been interested in this topic since the term "flying saucer" emerged after Arnold's sighting in 1947, as evidenced by the proliferation of television, books, movies, and podcasts today on the topic. The subject is deeply rooted in popular culture with its own themes, mythologies, and conspiracy theories. Capt Ruppelt, who was involved with three UFO investigations efforts, including being the initial leader of Project BLUE BOOK, noted that there would be spikes in reported sightings after official press events mentioning UFOs; suggesting that reports of sightings can influence the incidence of additional reported sightings.[124]

Alleged Bureaucratic Barriers

Alleged bureaucratic barriers including indifference, cognitive dissonance, lack of support or resources, and deliberate obstruction are also similarities. Some members of investigatory panels have claimed official obstruction, ranging from lack of access to senior decision-makers to insufficient staff and resources.

Insufficient Data and Information

Previous and current investigations have been challenged by insufficient data and information for intelligence and scientific analysis to resolve anomalous incidents. Insufficient data and information was compounded by inconsistent reporting and lack of continuity among investigations and investigative practices. Capt Ruppelt, the first director of Project BLUE BOOK, noted that the inability to collect the UFO's altitude, size, and speed was a recurring and significant obstacle to resolving cases.[125] A similar challenge remains today, even with the advancement in technology. Most UAP sightings have no data associated with them beyond an often vague narrative account; and when there is hard data, it is often incomplete or of poor quality. In terms of military reporting, the sensors on which UAP most frequently are captured are calibrated and optimized for combat. UAP are not routinely captured by exquisite, high-definition, multi-capability, intelligence, surveillance, and reconnaissance collection platforms— a threshold which is often required to successfully resolve a case.

Perceived Deception

There is a conviction among some Americans that the USG has conducted a deception operation to conceal the fact that it has recovered extraterrestrial spacecraft and alien beings as well as systematically exploited and reverse-engineered extraterrestrial technology.[126] This perception probably has been fueled by key UFO investigators' public comments. For example, J. Allen Hynek of Project BLUE BOOK, said that the USAF expected him to perform the role of debunker; and Capt Ruppelt, the first chief of BLUE BOOK, later wrote that he was expected to explain away every report and that the USAF sought to produce press stories in alignment with the USAF's position.[127]

Differences between 20th and 21st Century UAP Investigations

Decreased Public Trust

Polling data on public trust reflects Americans' changing views over time. According to the Pew Research Center, polling on this topic began in 1958, when about 75 percent of Americans trusted the USG "to do the right thing almost always or most of the time." Since 2007, however, that figure has not risen above 30 percent. This lack of trust probably has contributed to the belief held by some subset of the U.S. population that the USG has not been truthful regarding knowledge of extraterrestrial craft.[128]

Popular Culture

Though there were waves of public interest in UAP in popular culture during the Cold War, especially during the 1950s, AARO assesses that UAP content in popular culture is more pervasive now than ever. The speed of discovery, and the ubiquity of information available through the internet on the topic is unprecedented. Frequent exposure to the topic though traditional and social media has increased the number of Americans who believe that UAP are of extraterrestrial origin, based on a 2021 Gallup poll.[129]

Aside from hoaxes and forgeries, misinformation and disinformation is more prevalent and easier to disseminate now than ever before, especially with today's advanced photo, video, and computer generated imagery tools. Internet search and content recommendation algorithms serve to reinforce individuals' preconceptions and confirmation biases just as much as to help educate and inform.

SECTION VIII: Testing and Development of U.S. National Security and Space Programs Most Likely Accounted for Some Portion of UAP Sightings

Summary

We assess that the majority of UAP sightings in the earlier decades of UAP investigations were the result of misidentification of ordinary phenomena and objects, based on AARO's findings of its own cases to date and the findings of all past investigatory efforts. However, we assess that some portion of these misidentifications almost certainly were a result of the surge in new technologies that observers would have understandably reported as UFOs.

Along with these systems, a broad and varying technology industry emerged along with a network of highly secretive national laboratories across the United States to support these efforts. AARO's review of Project BLUE BOOK cases shows a spike in reported UAP sightings from 1952-1957 and another spike in 1960.[130] These reporting spikes most likely are attributed to observers unknowingly having witnessed new technological advancements and testing and reporting them as UFOs. The below examples represent formerly classified and sensitive programs that involved thousands of test flights, rocket launches, and extensive experimentation which AARO assess most likely were the cause of many UAP reports. AARO assesses that this common and understandable occurrence—the misidentification of new technologies for UAP—

39

is present today, such as in cases where rocket exhaust plumes, micro-satellite trains, and UAS systems with odd morphologies are reported as UAP.

The below examples represent a sample of the unclassified and declassified authentic national security programs that AARO assesses probably were associated with erroneous UAP reporting:

Manhattan Project (August 1942)

The U.S. effort to build an atomic bomb, the Manhattan Project, was named after the location of its initial offices in what became known as the Manhattan Engineer District at 270 Broadway, Manhattan, New York City. General Leslie R. Groves, head of the project, followed the custom of naming the U.S. Army Corps of Engineers' districts after the city in which they were located.[131] The secrecy surrounding the Manhattan Project and the establishment of several other national laboratories, such as Los Alamos National Laboratories, Lawrence Livermore National Laboratory, Sandia National Laboratories, Pacific Northwest National Laboratory, and Oak Ridge National Laboratory to support this effort probably contributed to the spike in reported UAP.[132]

V-173/XF5U-1 "Flying Pancake" (1942)

The V-173 aircraft flew for the first time on November 23, 1942.[133] It was believed that maintaining a uniform airflow over the wingspan—or "pancake" fuselage—would allow the aircraft to take off and land at exceptionally low speeds without sacrificing high-speed performance qualities that appealed to the USN for its fighter aircraft.[134] The V-173 could take off vertically, had a circular wing 23.3 feet in diameter, and could almost hover. The XF5U-1's design was largely similar to the V-173. However, the USN cancelled the project in 1948 in favor of a switch to turbojet engines.[135]

Project Mogul (1947-1949)

The U.S. Army Air Force Air Materiel Command operated Project Mogul between 1947 and 1949. The aim of this program was to secure intelligence on Soviet nuclear weapons testing and to provide an early warning mechanism for Soviet ballistic missiles. Specifically, Project Mogul scientists worked on developing high-altitude balloons that would carry sensors capable of detecting long-range sound waves from weapons tests or missiles traveling through the atmosphere. A crashed balloon associated with Project Mogul outside of Roswell, New Mexico, is assessed to be the source of early UFO claims.[136]

Project High Dive (1950s)

Project High Dive was a program that conducted tests on large balloons and used test dummies in its experimentation. The goal of this program was to research the effects on pilots when they ejected from aircraft, especially pilots' tolerance to deceleration from wind drag.[137]

40

Project Aquatone/Dragon Lady (1954)

President Eisenhower authorized Project Aquatone to develop the U-2 Dragon Lady, a high-altitude reconnaissance aircraft to collect intelligence on Soviet nuclear deployments. More than half of the UFO reports investigated in the 1950s and 1960s were assessed to be U.S. reconnaissance flights, according to a declassified CIA assessment on reconnaissance aircraft.[138] The report noted that UFO reports would spike when the U-2 was in flight, especially from airline pilots to Air Traffic Control. At that time, commercial flights typically flew below 20,000 feet while the U-2 flew at 60,000 feet. The report noted that when commercial pilots were flying east to west, with the sun below the horizon, the sunlight would illuminate the U-2.[139]

WS-117L/CORONA (Late 1956)

In 1956, the USAF initiated the WS-117L satellite reconnaissance program equipped with a film-return vehicle. Following the launch of Sputnik, the Eisenhower Administration made this program a high-priority. In February 1958, President Eisenhower decided the CIA would have the lead role in the program, called "CORONA," and that it would be jointly managed alongside the USAF. The CORONA program performed 140 launches between 1959 and 1972, with many returning film from space to the Earth for recovery.[140]

VZ-9AV Avrocar/Project Silver Bug (1958)

Canada initially led an effort to develop a supersonic, vertical takeoff and landing fighter-bomber in the early 1950s. A.V. Roe (Avro) Aircraft Limited (later Avro Canada) led the design for the concept, and this effort yielded the Avrocar, an aircraft with a circular shape that gave it a stereotypical "flying saucer" appearance.[141] Canada pulled its support when the project became too expensive. The U.S. Army and U.S. USAF took over the project in 1958 when Avro offered it to the USG, when it became known as "Project Silver Bug."[142] [143] Avro built two test vehicles that were designated as the VZ-9AV Avrocar, but the project was cancelled in December 1961 when the vehicle could not lift more than a few feet off the ground.[144] Project Silver Bug was declassified in 1997.[145]

Explorer 1 (January 1958)

The United States launched its first satellite, Explorer 1, into space on January 31, 1958. Explorer 1 carried a cosmic ray detector and was designed, built, and operated by the NASA Jet Propulsion Laboratory.[146]

Oxcart/A-12/SR-71 (1958)

President Eisenhower approved this CIA-led program to develop a successor to the U-2 spy plane in 1958, which became fully operational in 1965.[147] The U-2's successor, the A-12 OXCART sustained a speed of Mach 3.2 at 90,000 feet altitude.[148] By the time the A-12 was deployed by the CIA in 1967, CORONA satellites were being used to collect imagery of denied areas with less provocation than aircraft overflights.[149] In 1968, President Johnson ordered the retirement of the A-12 when it was replaced by the SR-71, which itself was a modified version of the A-12.[150]

41

Project Mercury (1958-1963)

Project Mercury, America's first human space program made six flights. The objectives of the program were to orbit a manned spacecraft around Earth, investigate humans' ability to function in space, and recover astronauts and spacecraft safely.[151]

TATTLETALE/GRAB (September 1960)

The United States was the first nation to deliver a reconnaissance satellite to space. This electronic intelligence (ELINT) satellite was developed by the Naval Research Laboratory in early 1958 under the code name "TATTLETALE" with the mission of intercepting Soviet radar signals.[152] The program later became known as GRAB (Galactic Radiation and Background), after public disclosure of the ELINT satellite project.[153] [154]

Project Gemini (1961-1966)

The Gemini program was a U.S. human spaceflight program that took place between the Mercury and Apollo programs. Similar to Project Mercury, Project Gemini spacecraft was launched using ballistic missiles that were designed to carry nuclear payloads.[155] Project Gemini conducted 12 missions.[156]

Project Apollo (1961-1972)

Project Apollo was a NASA human spaceflight program conducted after Project Mercury and Project Gemini.[157] Project Apollo totaled 14 missions, 11 spaceflights, and 12 astronauts walking on the moon.[158]

Poppy (1962-1977)

The successor to GRAB, Poppy was an ELINT satellite system developed by the National Research Laboratory that operated from 1962 to 1977 to collect Soviet radar emissions.[159] A total of seven Poppy missions were launched between December 1962 and December 1971.[160] The program was declassified in 2004.[161]

Gambit (1963-1971)

The National Reconnaissance Office (NRO) launched its first high-resolution photoreconnaissance satellite system in 1963, which became known by its codename, Gambit.[162] Two Gambit systems were developed: Gambit 1, initially launched in 1963, and Gambit 3, which was first launched in 1966.[163] The Gambit 1 satellite's exposed film was returned to Earth in reentry vehicles, or "buckets," that separated from the satellite, fell through the atmosphere and descended by parachute until obtained by USAF aircraft at about 15,000 feet altitude.[164] Gambit was declassified in 2011.

Hexagon (1971- 1986)

Similar to Gambit, Hexagon was an NRO photoreconnaissance satellite system. It was launched in 1971 to conduct wide-area searches of denied territory.[165] From 1971-1986, 19 missions collected imagery over 877 million square miles of the Earth's surface.[166] The

42

Hexagon system was the last satellite employing film reentry vehicles.[167] Hexagon was declassified in 2011.[168]

Space Transportation System/Space Shuttle (1972 - 2011)

The Space Shuttle program was NASA's fourth human spaceflight program and was comprised of the first reusable spacecraft to carry humans into Earth's orbit.[169] The space shuttle fleet—Columbia, Challenger, Discovery, Atlantis, and Endeavour—flew 135 missions, serviced the Hubble space telescope, and helped construct the International Space Station.[170] The first shuttle launch, Columbia, was conducted on April 12, 1981.[171]

HAVE Blue/F-117A Nighthawk/TACIT Blue (1975)

The Defense Advanced Research Project Agency (DARPA) oversaw the development of HAVE Blue in the mid-1970s, which was the first practical, combat-stealth aircraft. HAVE Blue completed its first test flight in 1977, and the success of this program led the USAF to later produce the F-117A Nighthawk, as well as the TACIT Blue aircraft. The HAVE Blue, F-117A Nighthawk, and TACIT Blue programs laid the foundations for the later development of the B-2 stealth bomber.[172]

Advanced Technology Bomber/B-2 Spirit (1980)

The B-2 is a USAF low-observable stealth bomber capable of delivering conventional and nuclear payloads. It uses a combination of reduced infrared, acoustic, and electromagnetic signatures. It was first publicly displayed on November 22, 1988 in Palmdale, California and conducted its first flight on July 17, 1989. The first aircraft was delivered on December 17, 1993.[173]

Strategic Defense Initiative (March 1983)

At the initiative of President Ronald Reagan, the Strategic Defense Initiative Organization was established in 1984 to explore a multi-layered strategic defense against ballistic missiles; this program involved research into space-based and ground-based systems including laser and interceptor missiles. This intensive research effort involved national laboratories and academia. Some of the technologies researched were determined to be years from development, and funding was reduced. The program ended in 1993 and was replaced by the Ballistic Missile Defense Organization.[174]

Advent of Unmanned Aerial Vehicles 1980s-Present

The research and development, flight testing, evaluation, deployment, and the operation of drones—Unmanned Aerial Systems (UAS), Unmanned Aerial Vehicles (UAV), Remotely Piloted Aircraft (RPA), and Remotely Piloted Aircraft Systems (RPAS)—almost certainly resulted in reported sightings of UAP. Some of these systems had a "saucer" or triangle-shaped appearance and were capable of loitering aloft.

The USG acquired and operated a number of systems for a range of missions including intelligence, surveillance, reconnaissance, and strike, among others. The below systems

43

represent a sample of those that have been operationally deployed since the 1994 Bosnia conflict and subsequently employed in counterterrorism operations around the world.[175] Since then, their form and use have spread to civil and commercial applications.

GNAT 750

The GNAT 750 was developed in the late 1980s by General Atomics Aeronautical Systems, Inc. The prototype served as the basis for a more advanced design under DARPA.[176] It was first used in 1994 during the Bosnia conflict where satellites were not optimized to collect for extended times over such small areas and where the airspace was heavily defended by capable anti-aircraft missile systems.[177]

Predator

The Predator system, also built by General Atomics Aeronautical Systems, Inc., was based on the GNAT-750.[178] It was initially a joint USN and U.S. Army project but transitioned to the USAF in 1996.[179] It was known as the RQ-1.[180] The system possessed synthetic aperture radar, electro-optical, and infrared sensors. [181] It was used to support United Nations and North Atlantic Treaty Organization efforts in Bosnia and was widely used in counterterrorism operations.[182] It became a platform with a wide array of technical capabilities that performed a variety of missions—such as close air support, combat search and rescue, precision strike, convoy/raid over watch, target development and terminal air guidance.[183] The USAF retired the fleet in 2018.[184]

Reaper

General Atomics Aeronautical Systems, Inc. also built the MQ-9 Reaper—a newer, larger version of the MQ-1 Predator UAV.[185] This platform is faster, equipped with more advanced sensors, can carry more munitions than the Predator, and can be easily tailored with a variety of mission-specific capabilities.[186] The system requires a pilot to control the aircraft and an aircrew member to operate the sensors and weapons.[187] [188] It has an operational altitude of 50,000 feet.[189] The aircraft is operated out of a variety of locations worldwide, including Creech Air Force Base (AFB) in Nevada.[190]

Dark Star

The RQ-3 Dark Star was a remote pilot-assisted stealth system intended to conduct reconnaissance missions in high-threat areas. Lockheed Martin, Boeing, and DARPA developed Dark Star in the mid-to-late 1990s.[191] It never entered production, but the research conducted on Dark Star led to subsequent advances used on other platforms. Some observers asserted that Dark Star resembled a flying saucer with long narrow wings.[192]

It was designed to be fully autonomous from its launch, mission engagement, and return. It used satellite links to transmit sensor data. The first prototype flew in 1996, but crashed a month later on its second flight. The system completed five test flights before DoD terminated the program in 1999 due to cost and instability problems.[193]

44

Polecat

Lockheed Martin's Advanced Development Program organization, also known as "Skunk Works" developed the P-175 Polecat UAV to better understand the flight dynamics of tailless, bat-wing- shaped, 90-foot wingspan high-altitude UAV, including the next generation of structural composite materials and configurations.[194] The Polecat made its first flight in 2005, and Lockheed Martin disclosed its existence in the Farnborough Airshow in 2006.[195]

Sentinel

The RQ-170 Sentinel is a UAV developed by Lockheed Martin's Skunk Works for the USAF.[196] It is a low observable platform with a variety of intelligence, surveillance, and reconnaissance payloads. The Sentinel is operated out of Creech AFB and the Tonopah Test Range in Nevada.[197]

Global Hawk

Built by Northrop Grumman, the RQ-4 Global Hawk is the largest UAS in operation by the USAF.[198] It can fly at 65,000 feet more than 34 hours and is also capable of loitering at 60,000 feet while monitoring almost 58,000 square miles.[199] The aircraft is currently fielded in three different models.[200]

SECTION IX: Conclusion

To date, AARO has not discovered any empirical evidence that any sighting of a UAP represented off-world technology or the existence a classified program that had not been properly reported to Congress. Investigative efforts determined that most sightings were the result of misidentification of ordinary objects and phenomena. Although many UAP reports remain unsolved, AARO assesses that if additional, quality data were available, most of these cases also could be identified and resolved as ordinary objects or phenomena.

This report represents Volume I of AARO's HR2. Volume II will be published in accordance with the date established in Section 6802 of the National Defense Authorization Act for Fiscal Year 2023 (FY23) and will provide additional analysis on information not yet secured and analyzed, interviews not yet conducted, and additional avenues of investigation not yet completed by the date of the publication of Volume I.

[1] Anjali Nandan, "Eyewitness Testimony: A Psychological and Legal Perspective," *Journal of Positive School of Psychology*, 2022; Biswa Prakesh Nayak & H. Khajuria, "Eyewitness Testimony: Probative Value in the Criminal Justice System," *Egyptian Journal of Forensic Science*, 2019; Stephen L. Chew, "Myth: Eyewitness Testimony is the Best Kind of Evidence," Association for Psychological Science, 2018; Fangting Liu, "The Reliability of Eyewitness Testimony," from the Proceedings of the 2021 International Conference on Public Relations and Social Sciences, Atlantis Press, 2021.

[2] Daniel Khaneman, "Thinking Fast and Slow," Farrar, Strauss, and Giroux, 2013; Helen Lee, "Don't Let Anchoring Bias Weigh Down Your Judgment," *Harvard Business Review*, August 30, 2022; Richard J, Heuer, Jr., "Psychology of Intelligence Analysis," Novinka Books, 1999; Drake Baer, "Kahneman: Your Confirmation Bias Acts Like an Optical Illusion," *The Cut*, January 13, 2017; Ben Yagoda, "The Cognitive Bias Tricking Your Brain," *The Atlantic*, September 2018.

[3] https://military-history.fandom.com/wikiProject-Sign; Connors, Wendy, *Project Blue Book*

[4] Edward J. Ruppelt, *The Report on Unidentified Flying Objects* (Doubleday, 1956), https://ia801304.us.archive.org/22/items/FritjofCapraTheTurningPoint/Edward%20J%20Ruppelt%20-%20The%20Report%20on%20Unidentified%20Flying%20Objects.pdf

[5] Gerald K. Haines, "CIA's Role in the Study of UFOs, 1947-90," *Studies in Intelligence*, Vol 1, No. 1, (1997), pp. 67-84.

[6] Russell Lee, "1947: Year of the Flying Saucer," June 24, 2022, https://www.airandsapce.si.edu/stories/editorial/1947-year-flying-saucer

[7] Hector Quintanilla, Jr., "The Investigation of UFOs," *Studies in Intelligence*, Vol. 10, No. 4 (Fall 1966), pp. 95-110, https://catalog.archives.gov/id/7282832

[8] Edward J. Ruppelt, *The Report on Unidentified Flying Objects* (Doubleday, 1956), https://ia801304.us.archive.org/22/items/FritjofCapraTheTurningPoint/Edward%20J%20Ruppelt%20-%20The%20Report%20on%20Unidentified%20Flying%20Objects.pdf; USAF https://www.esd.whs.mil/Portals/54/Documents/FOID/Reading%20Room/UFOsandUAPs/2d_a_1.pdf

[9] J. Marker, "Public Interest in UFOs Persists 50 Years after Project Blue Book Termination," 2019; Hector Quintanilla, Jr., "The Investigation of UFOs," *Studies in Intelligence*, Vol. 10, No. 4 (Fall 1966), 95-110.

46

[10] Hector Quintanilla, Jr., "UFOs: An Air Force Dilemma" (unpublished manuscript, 1974). https://ia902205.us.archive.org/28/items/ufos-an-air-force-dilemma/quintanilla.pdf; Edward J. Ruppelt, *The Report on Unidentified Flying Objects* (Doubleday, 1956), https://ia801304.us.archive.org/22/items/FritjofCapraTheTurningPoint/Edward%20J%20Ruppelt%20-%20The%20Report%20on%20Unidentified%20Flying%20Objects.pdf

[11] National Archives and Records Administration, https://www.archives.gov/news/articles/project-blue-book-50th-anniversary; Edward J. Ruppelt, *The Report on Unidentified Flying Objects* (Doubleday, 1956). https://ia801304.us.archive.org/22/items/FritjofCapraTheTurningPoint/Edward%20J%20Ruppelt%20-%20The%20Report%20on%20Unidentified%20Flying%20Objects.pdf

[12] Edward J. Ruppelt, *The Report on Unidentified Flying Objects* (Doubleday, 1956). https://ia801304.us.archive.org/22/items/FritjofCapraTheTurningPoint/Edward%20J%20Ruppelt%20-%20The%20Report%20on%20Unidentified%20Flying%20Objects.pdf

[13] Ibid.

[14] Ibid.

[15] Gerald K. Haines, "CIA's Role in the Study of UFOs, 1947-90," *Studies in Intelligence*, Vol 1, No. 1, (1997), pp. 67-84; USAF https://www.secretsdeclassified.af.mil/Portals/67/documents/AFD-110719-005.pdf?ver=2016-07-19-142520-690; Project Grudge Report, https://www.academia.edu/43389931/Project_GRUDGE_Report_1949USA

[16] Gerald K. Haines, "CIA's Role in the Study of UFOs, 1947-90," *Studies in Intelligence*, Vol 1, No. 1, (1997), pp. 67-84; Mihm, S., "US Government Has Been Dancing Around UFOs for 75 Years." *The Washington Post*. 2023, https://www.washingtonpost.com/business/us-government-has-been-dancing-around-ufos-for-75-years/2023/02/22/7ce50280-b2c4-11ed-94a0-512954d75716_story.html

[17] https://www.archives.gov/news/articles/project-blue-book-50th-anniversary

[18] Edward J. Ruppelt, *The Report on Unidentified Flying Objects* (Doubleday, 1956). https://ia801304.us.archive.org/22/items/FritjofCapraTheTurningPoint/Edward%20J%20Ruppelt%20-%20The%20Report%20on%20Unidentified%20Flying%20Objects.pdf.

[19] Ibid.

47

[20] Ibid.

[21] Ibid.

[22] Ibid.

[23] Ibid.

[24] Hector Quintanilla Jr., "The Investigation of UFOs," *Studies in Intelligence*, Vol. 10, No. 4 (Fall 1966), pp. 95-110, https://catalog.archives.gov/id/7282832; U.S. Congress, House of Representatives; https://history.house.gov/Blog/Detail/15032395730

[25] Ibid.

[26] Gerald K. Haines, "CIA's Role in the Study of UFOs, 1947-90," *Studies in Intelligence*, Vol. 1, No. 1, (1997), pp. 67-84; https://www.cia.gov/readingroom/docs/DOC_0000838058.pdf

[27] Ibid.

[28] Ibid.

[29] "The Robertson Panel Report," https://www.cia.gov/readingroom/document/cia-rdp81r00100030027-0

[30] Hector Quintanilla, Jr., "The Investigation of UFOs," *Studies in Intelligence*, Vol. 10, No. 4 (Fall 1966), pp. 95-110, https://catalog.archives.gov/id/7282832; Gerald K. Haines, "CIA's Role in the Study of UFOs, 1947-90," *Studies in Intelligence*, Vol. 1, No. 1, (1997), pp. 67-84; https://www.cia.gov/readingroom/docs/DOC_0000838058.pdf

[31] "The Robertson Panel Report", https://www.cia.gov/readingroom/document/cia-rdp81r00100030027-0; Gerald K. Haines, "CIA's Role in the Study of UFOs, 1947-90," *Studies in Intelligence*, Vol. 1, No. 1, (1997), pp. 67-84; https://www.cia.gov/readingroom/docs/DOC_0000838058.pdf

[32] Ibid.

[33] *The Durant Report,* https://www.cia.gov/readingroom/document/cia-rdp81r00100030027-0; Gerald K. Haines, "CIA's Role in the Study of UFOs, 1947-90," Studies in Intelligence, Vol. 1, No. 1, (1997), pp. 67-84; https://www.cia.gov/readingroom/docs/DOC_0000838058.pdf

[34] Ibid.

[35] National Archives and Records Administration (NARA), https://www.archives.gov/research/military/air-force/ufos#bluebk; NARA, https://www.archives.gov/news/articles/project-blue-book-50th-anniversary; Department of the Air Force, Project Blue Book, (February 1, 1966); USAF, https://www.esd.whs.mil/Portals/54/Documents/FOID/Reading%20Room/UFOsandUAPs/2d_af 1.pdf; Hector Quintanilla, Jr., "The Investigation of UFOs," *Studies in Intelligence*, Vol. 10, No. 4 (Fall1966), pp. 95-110., https://catalog.archives.gov/id/7282832; Hector Quintanilla, Jr., "UFOs: An Air Force Dilemma" (unpublished manuscript, 1974); https://ia902205.us.archive.org/28/items/ufos-an-air-force-dilemma/quintanilla.pdf; Edward J. Ruppelt, *The Report on Unidentified Flying Objects* (Doubleday, 1956), https://ia801304.us.archive.org/22/items/FritjofCapraTheTurningPoint/Edward%20J%20Ruppelt %20-%20The%20Report%20on%20Unidentified%20Flying%20Objects.pdf; Gerald K. Haines, "CIA's Role in the Study of UFOs, 1947-90," *Studies in Intelligence*, Vol. 1, No. 1.

[36] National Archives and Records Administration (NARA), https://www.archives.gov/research/military/air-force/ufos#bluebk; NARA, https://www.archives.gov/news/articles/project-blue-book-50th-anniversary; Department of the Air Force, *Project Blue Book*, (February 1, 1966), USAF, https://www.esd.whs.mil/Portals/54/Documents/FOID/Reading%20Room/UFOsandUAPs/2d_af 1.pdf; Hector Quintanilla, Jr., "The Investigation of UFOs," *Studies in Intelligence*, Vol. 10, No. 4 (Fall1966), pp. 95-110., https://catalog.archives.gov/id/7282832; Hector Quintanilla, Jr., "UFOs: An Air Force Dilemma" (unpublished manuscript, 1974); https://ia902205.us.archive.org/28/items/ufos-an-air-force-dilemma/quintanilla.pdf.

[37] Department of Defense, Press Release, 17 December 1969.

[38] National Archives and Records Administration (NARA), https://www.archives.gov/research/military/air-force/ufos#bluebk; NARA, https://www.archives.gov/news/articles/project-blue-book-50th-anniversary.

[39] National Archives and Records Administration (NARA), https://www.archives.gov/research/military/air-force/ufos#bluebk; NARA, https://www.archives.gov/news/articles/project-blue-book-50th-anniversary; Department of the Air Force, *Project Blue Book*, (February 1, 1966), USAF, https://www.esd.whs.mil/Portals/54/Documents/FOID/Reading%20Room/UFOsandUAPs/2d_af 1.pdf; Hector Quintanilla, Jr., "The Investigation of UFOs," *Studies in Intelligence*, Vol. 10, No. 4 (Fall1966), pp. 95-110., https://catalog.archives.gov/id/7282832; Hector Quintanilla, Jr., "UFOs: An Air Force Dilemma" (unpublished manuscript, 1974);

https://ia902205.us.archive.org/28/items/ufos-an-air-force-dilemma/quintanilla.pdf; Edward J. Ruppelt, *The Report on Unidentified Flying Objects* (Doubleday, 1956), https://ia801304.us.archive.org/22/items/FritjofCapraTheTurningPoint/Edward%20J%20Ruppelt%20-%20The%20Report%20on%20Unidentified%20Flying%20Objects.pdf; Gerald K. Haines, "CIA's Role in the Study of UFOs, 1947-90," *Studies in Intelligence*, Vol. 1, No. 1.

[40] Gerald K. Haines, "CIA's Role in the Study of UFOs, 1947-90," *Studies in Intelligence*, Vol. 1, No. 1, (1997), pp. 67-84, https://www.cia.gov/readingroom/docs/DOC_0000838058.pdf

[41] Ibid.

[42] Ibid.

[43] Ibid.

[44] "The Condon Report," https://apps.dtic.mil/sti/pdfs/AD0680976.pdf, https://files.ncas.org/condon; Dr. Edward U. Condon, *Scientific Study of Unidentified Flying Objects* (Bantam, 1968)., University of Colorado, Boulder, https://www.colorado.edu/coloradan/2021/11/05/condon-report-cu-boulders-historic-ufo-stu

[45] Ibid.

[46] Ibid.

[47] Ibid.

[48] Ibid.

[49] Ibid.

[50] The National Academy of Sciences Panel Assessment of the Condon Report; https://www.apps.dtic.mil/sti/pdfs/ADO688541.pdf

[51] Ibid.

[52] Richard C. Henry, "UFOs and NASA," Journal of Scientific Exploration, Vol. 2, No. 2, (1988). https://henry.pha.jhu.edu/ufosNASA.pdf; *The Washington Post*, https://www.washingtonpost.com/archive/politics/1977/04/30/ufo-over-georgia-jimmy-loggedone/080ef1c3-6ff3-41a9-a1e4-a37c54b5cbca/

[53] Presidential Papers of the United States, https://www.govinfo.gov/content/pkg/PPP-1995-book2/html/PPP-1995-book2-doc-pg1813-2.htm; "Bill Clinton Phones Home on Aliens," Politico, Tal Kopan, April 3, 2014; *The Washington Post*, https://www.washingtonpost.com/news/the-fix/wp/2016/04/08/the-long-strange-history-of-johnpodestas-space-alien-obsession/; *New York Times*, https://www.nytimes.com/2016/05/11/us/politics/hillary-clinton-aliens.html

[54] Government Accountability Office, https://www.gao.gov/assets/nsiad-95-187.pdf

[55] U.S. Air Force, *The Roswell Report: Fact versus Fiction in the New Mexico Desert* (Government Printing Office, 1995), https://apps.dtic.mil/sti/pdfs/ADA326148.pdf

[56] Ibid.

[57] U.S. Air Force, https://www.af.mil/The-Roswell-Report; USAF, *The Roswell Report: Case Closed* (Government Printing Office, 1994), https://media.defense.gov/2010/Oct/27/2001330219/-1/-1/0/AFD-101027-030.pdf

[58] Ibid.

[59] U.S. Air Force, https://www.af.mil/The-Roswell-Report; USAF, *The Roswell Report: Case Closed* (Government Printing Office, 1994), https://media.defense.gov/2010/Oct/27/2001330219/-1/-1/0/AFD-101027-030.pdf; U.S. Air Force, *The Roswell Report: Fact versus Fiction in the New Mexico Desert* (Government Printing Office, 1995), https://apps.dtic.mil/sti/pdfs/ADA326148.pdf

[60] Government Accountability Office, https://www.gao.gov/assets/nsiad-95-187.pdf

[61] Info Memo, From Former Defense Intelligence Agency Director to the Undersecretary of Defense for Acquisition, Technology, and Logistics, December 1, 2010.

[62] Info Memo, From Former Defense Intelligence Agency Director to the Undersecretary of Defense for Acquisition, Technology, and Logistics, December 1, 2010.

[63] Review of Report from a private sector organization 1, July 30, 2009.

[64] Ibid.

51

[65] Defense Intelligence Agency, https://www.dia.mil/FOIA/FOIA-Electronic-Reading-Room; *New York Times*, https://www.nytimes.com/2017/12/16/us/politics/pentagon-program-ufo-harry-reid.html.

[66] Memorandum, from the Under Secretary of Defense James Clapper to the Deputy Secretary of Defense, 17 November 2009.

[67] Review of Report from a private sector organization, July 30 2009.

[68] Ibid.

[69] Department of Defense, https://www.defense.gov/News/Releases/Release/Article/2314065/establishment-of-unidentifiedaerial-phenomena-task-force/

[70] AARO discussions with UAPTF leadership.

[71] Office of the Director of National Intelligence, *Preliminary Assessment: Unidentified Aerial Phenomena, Preliminary Assessment: Unidentified Aerial Phenomena*

[72] Department of Defense, https://www.defense.gov/News/Releases/Release/Article/2853121/dod-announces-theestablishment-of-the-airborne-object-identification-and-manag/; DoD, https://media.defense.gov/2021/Nov/23/2002898596/-1/-1/0/ESTABLISHMENT-OF-THEAIRBORNE-OBJECT-IDENTIFICATION-AND-MANAGEMENT-SYNCHRONIZATIONGROUP PDF

[73] Ibid.

[74] National Aeronautics and Space Administration, https://science.nasa.gov/uap; National Aeronautics and Space Administration, https://science.nasa.gov/science-red/s3fspublic/atoms/files/UAPIST%20Terms%20of%20Reference%20-%20Signed.pdf; National Aeronautics and Space Administration, https://www.nasa.gov/feature/nasa-announces-unidentified-anomalous-phenomena-study-teammembers/

[75] Department of Defense, https://www.defense.gov/News/Releases/Release/Article/3100053/dod-announces-theestablishment-of-the-all-domain-anomaly-resolution-office/

[76] Office of the Director of National Intelligence, *2022 Annual Report on Unidentified Aerial Phenomena.*

[77] P.A. Sturrock, et. al., "Physical Evidence Related to UFO Reports: The Proceedings of a Workshop Held at the Pocantico Conference Center, Tarrytown, New York, September 29 - October 4, 1997," *Journal of Scientific Exploration*, Vol. 12, No. 2, (1998). http://www.jse.com/ufo_reports/Sturrock/toc.html; Stanford University https://www.sciencedaily.com/releases/1998/07/980701082300.htm

[78] United Kingdom National Archives. https://cdn.nationalarchives.gov.uk/documents/briefing-guide-12-07-12.pdf; Gerald K. Haines, "CIA's Role in the Study of UFOs, 1947-90," *Studies in Intelligence*, Vol. 1, No. 1, (1997), pp. 67-84; https://www.cia.gov/readingroom/docs/DOC_0000838058.pdf

[79] Department of National Defense, https://s3.documentcloud.org/documents/21885184/documents-obtained-through-access-toinformation-ufo-files.pdf; CTV News; https://www.ctvnews.ca/sci-tech/document-reveals-first-known-canadian-ufo-study-in-nearly-30-years-now-underway-1.6293124

[80] University of Ottawa, https://biblio.uottawa.ca/atom/index.php/project-second-story https://biblio.uottawa.ca/atom/index.php/project-second-story-defence-research-board-meetingminutes; Mathew Hayes, "A History of Canada's UFO Investigation, 1950-1995," Dissertation Submitted to the Committee on Graduate Studies in Partial Fulfillment of the Requirements for the Degree of Doctor of Philosophy in the Faculty of Arts and Science.

[81] Rod Tennyson, University of Toronto Institute for Aerophysics Studies, "1960s: Dr. Gordon Peterson Establishes the UTIAS UFO Project; https://www.utias.utoronto.ca/2018/08/15/1960s-dr-gordon-patterson-establishes-the-utias-ufo-project; Timothy Good, "Above Top Secret," William Morrow & Company, 1988; Matthew Hayes, "Then the Saucers Do Exist?": UFOs, the Practice of Conspiracy, and the Case of Wilbert Smith," Journal of Canadian Studies, University of Toronto Press, Volume 52, Number 3, Fall 2017, pp. 665-696

[82] CNES, https://cnes.fr/en/web/CNES-en/5866-geipan-uap-investigation-opens-its-files.php; https://cnes-geipan.fr.en.node/5891

[83] National Archives and Records Administration, https://www.archives.gov/news/articles/project-blue-book-50th-anniversary; Edward J. Ruppelt, *The Report on Unidentified Flying Objects* (Doubleday, 1956). https://ia801304.us.archive.org/22/items/FritjofCapraTheTurningPoint/Edward%20J%20Ruppelt%20-%20The%20Report%20on%20Unidentified%20Flying%20Objects.pdf

84 AARO case files

85 AARO case files

86 AARO case files

87 AARO case files

88 AARO case files

89 AARO case files

90 AARO case files

91 AARO case files

92 AARO case files

93 AARO case files

94 AARO case files

95 AARO case files

96 AARO case files

97 AARO case files

98 AARO case files

99 AARO case files

100 AARO case files

101 AARO case files

102 AARO case files

103 AARO case files

[104] AARO case files

[105] AARO case files

[106] AARO case files

[107] AARO case files

[108] AARO case files

[109] AARO case files

[110] AARO case files

[111] AARO case files

[112] AARO case files

[113] AARO case files

[114] AARO case files

[115] AARO case files

[116] Senator Harry Reid Letter to Deputy Secretary of Defense, William Lynn III; Memorandum, from the Under Secretary of Defense James Clapper to the Deputy Secretary of Defense, 17 November 2009; program documentation from ARRO case files

[117] AARO case files

[118] Program documentation, from AARO case files

[119] Senator Harry Reid Letter to Deputy Secretary of Defense, William Lynn III; Memorandum, from the Under Secretary of Defense James Clapper to the Deputy Secretary of Defense, 17 November 2009.

[120] AARO case files

[121] AARO case files

[122] AARO case files

[123] AARO case files

[124] Edward J. Ruppelt, *The Report on Unidentified Flying Objects* (Doubleday, 1956). https://ia801304.us.archive.org/22/items/FritjofCapraTheTurningPoint/Edward%20J%20Ruppelt%20-%20The%20Report%20on%20Unidentified%20Flying%20Objects.pdf. Page 93.

[125] Ibid, page 91.

[126] J. Allen Hyneck, "The UFO Experience," Da Capo Press, 1977; Edward J. Ruppelt, *The Report on Unidentified Flying Objects* (Doubleday, 1956),

[127] Ibid.

[128] Pew Research Center, "Public Trust in Government: 1958-2022," June 6, 2022. https://www.pewresearch.org/politics/2022/06/06/public-trust-in-government-1958-2022/

[129] "Do Americans Believe in UFOs," Gallup, https://www.news/gallup/com/poll/350096/americans-beleive-ufos.aspx

[130] National Archives and Records Administration, https://www.archives.gov/research/military/air-force/ufos#bluebk; National Archives and Records Administration, https://www.archives.gov/news/articles/project-blue-book-50th-anniversary; National Archives and Records Administration, https://www.youtube.com/watch?v=UlmwakUTo3M; Department of the Air Force, *Project Blue Book*, (February 1, 1966), USAF, https://www.esd.whs.mil/Portals/54/Documents/FOID/Reading%20Room/UFOsandUAPs/2d_af 1.pdf; Hector Quintanilla, Jr., "The Investigation of UFOs," *Studies in Intelligence*, Vol. 10, No. 4 (Fall1966), pp. 95-110., https://catalog.archives.gov/id/7282832; Hector Quintanilla, Jr., "UFOs: An Air Force Dilemma" (unpublished manuscript, 1974); https://ia902205.us.archive.org/28/items/ufos-an-air-force-dilemma/quintanilla.pdf; Hector Quintanilla, Jr., "UFOs: An Air Force Dilemma" (unpublished manuscript, 1974); https://ia902205.us.archive.org/28/items/ufos-an-air-force-dilemma/quintanilla.pdf; Edward J. Ruppelt, *The Report on Unidentified Flying Objects* (Doubleday, 1956), https://ia801304.us.archive.org/22/items/FritjofCapraTheTurningPoint/Edward%20J%20Ruppelt%20-%20The%20Report%20on%20Unidentified%20Flying%20Objects.pdf; Gerald K. Haines, "CIA's Role in the Study of UFOs, 1947-90," *Studies in Intelligence*, Vol. 1, No. 1

[131] Department of Energy (DoE), https://www.osti.gov/opennet/manhattan-project-history/Events/1945/trinity.htm, Leslie Groves, *Now It Can Be Told* (Harper, 1962). Richard Rhodes, *The Making of the Atomic Bomb* (Simon and Shuster, 1986), Kai Bird and Martin J. Sherwin

[132] Department of Energy (DoE) https://www.osti.gov/opennet/manhattan-project-history/Events/1945/trinity.htm; Leslie Groves, *Now It Can Be Told* (Harper, 1962); Richard Rhodes, *The Making of the Atomic Bomb* (Simon and Shuster, 1986).

[133] Norman Polmar, "The Pancake that Didn't Fly," *Naval History Magazine*, Volume 33, Number 3, (June 2019); https://www.usni.org/magazines/naval-history-magazine/2019/june/pancake-didnt-fly

[134] National Air and Space Museum, https://airandspace.si.edu/collection-objects/vought-v-173-flying-pancake/nasm_A19610120000; Norman Polmar, "The Pancake that Didn't Fly," *Naval History Magazine*, Volume 33, Number 3, (June 2019); https://www.usni.org/magazines/naval-history-magazine/2019/june/pancake-didnt-fly

[135] Ibid.

[136] U.S. Air Force, *The Roswell Report: Fact versus Fiction in the New Mexico Desert* (Government Printing Office, 1995); https://apps.dtic.mil/sti/pdfs/ADA326148.pdf; U.S. Air Force, *The Roswell Report: Case Closed* (Government Printing Office, 1995), https://media.defense.gov/2010/Oct/27/2001330219/-1/-1/0/AFD-101027-030.pdf

[137] National Aeronautics and Space Administration, https://history.nasa.gov/afspbio/part4-4.htm; U.S. Air Force, *The Roswell Report: Case Closed* (Government Printing Office, 1995), https://media.defense.gov/2010/Oct/27/2001330219/-1/-1/0/AFD-101027-030.pdf; U.S. Air Force, https://www.secretsdeclassified.af.mil/News/Photos/igphoto/2000345085/

[138] Gregory W. Pedlow and Donald E. Welzenbach, *The CIA and the U-2 Program, 1954-1974* (CIA Center for the Study of Intelligence, 1998), https://www.cia.gov/resources/csi/books-monographs/the-cia-and-the-u-2-program-1954-1974/; Gregory W. Pedlow and Donald E. Welzenbach, *The Central Intelligence Agency and Overhead; Reconnaissance Program, The U-2 and Oxcart Programs 1954-1974* (CIA History Staff, 1992), https://www.archives.gov/files/declassification/iscap/pdf/2014-004-doc01.pdf; Central Intelligence Agency, https://www.cia.gov/readingroom/docs/CIA-RDP62B00844R000200070131-1.pdf; Central Intelligence Agency,

57

https://irp.fas.org/program/collect/u2.pdf; National Security Agency, https://nsarchive2.gwu.edu/NSAEBB/NSAEBB54/docs/doc_40.PDF

[139] Ibid.

[140] Bruce Berkowitz, *A Brief History of the NRO (NRO Center for the Study of National Reconnaissance*, 2018, https://www.nro.gov/Portals/65/documents/history/csnr/programs/NRO_Brief_History.pdf; National Reconnaissance Office, https://www.nro.gov/History-and-Studies/Center-for-the-Study-of-National-Reconnaissance/The-CORONA-Program/; Dwayne Day, et. al., eds., *Eye in the Sky: The Story of the Corona Spy Satellites* (Smithsonian, 1998)

[141] U.S. Air Force, https://www.nationalmuseum.af.mil/Visit/Museum-Exhibits/Fact-Sheets/Display/Article/195801/avro-canada-vz-9av-avrocar/

[142] Ibid.

[143] American Heritage Center, "Flying Saucers—For Real! The Papers of Jack D. Pickett," https://ahcwyo.org/2022/04/04/flying-saucers-for-real-the-papers-of-jack-d-pickett/

[144] U.S. Air Force, https://www.nationalmuseum.af.mil/Visit/Museum-Exhibits/Fact-Sheets/Display/Article/195801/avro-canada-vz-9av-avrocar/

[145] American Heritage Center, "Flying Saucers—For Real! The Papers of Jack D, Pickett," https://ahcwyo.org/2022/04/04/flying-saucers-for-real-the-papers-of-jack-d-pickett/

[146] National Aeronautics and Space Administration, https://www.jpl.nasa.gov/missions/explorer-1

[147] National Security Archive, https://nsarchive2.gwu.edu/NSAEBB/NSAEBB74/

[148] Central Intelligence Agency, https://www.cia.gov/legacy/museum/exhibit/a-12-oxcart/

[149] Central Intelligence Agency, https://www.cia.gov/legacy/museum/exhibit/a-12-oxcart/; National Security Agency Archive, https://nsarchive2.gwu.edu/NSAEBB/NSAEBB74/

[150] Ibid.

[151] National Air and Space Museum, https://airandspace.si.edu/stories/editorial/what-was-mercury-program

[152] Robert A. McDonald and Sharon K. Moreno, *Raising the Periscope: Grab and Poppy: America's Early ELINT Satellites* (NRO History Office, 2005). https://www.nro.gov/Portals/65/documents/history/csnr/programs/docs/prog-hist-03.pdf

[153] Robert A. McDonald and Sharon K. Moreno, *Raising the Periscope: Grab and Poppy: America's Early ELINT Satellites* (NRO History Office, 2005). https://www.nro.gov/Portals/65/documents/history/csnr/programs/docs/prog-hist-03.pdf; U.S. Naval Research Laboratory, https://www.nrl.navy.mil/Media/News/Article/3074375/grab-i-first-operational-intelligence-satellite/

[154] Ibid.

[155] National Air and Space Museum, https://airandspace.si.edu/stories/editorial/what-was-gemini-program

[156] National Aeronautics and Space Administration, https://www.nasa.gov/gemini/; National Air and Space Museum, https://airandspace.si.edu/stories/editorial/what-was-gemini-program

[157] National Archives and Records Administration, Kennedy Library, https://www.jfklibrary.org/learn/about-jfk/historic-speeches/address-to-joint-session-of-congress-may-25-1961

[158] National Air and Space Museum, https://airandspace.si.edu/explore/topics/space/apollo-program; National Aeronautics and Space Administration, https://www.nasa.gov/learning-resources/for-kids-and-students/what-was-the-apollo-program-grades-5-8/; National Aeronautics and Space Administration, https://www.nasa.gov/specials/apollo50th/missions.html

[159] Robert A. McDonald and Sharon K. Moreno, *Raising the Periscope: Grab and Poppy: America's Early ELINT Satellites* (NRO History Office, 2005), https://www.nro.gov/Portals/65/documents/history/csnr/programs/docs/prog-hist-03.pdf

[160] Bruce Berkowitz, "A Brief History of the NRO" (NRO Center for the Study of National https://www.nro.gov/Portals/65/documents/history/csnr/programs/NRO_Brief_History.pdf

[161] Ibid.

[162] National Reconnaissance Office, https://www.nro.gov/Portals/65/documents/history/csnr/gambhex/Docs/GAM_1_Fact_sheet.pdf

59

[163] National Reconnaissance Office, https://www.nro.gov/About-NRO/history/more-historical-programs/

[164] National Museum of the United States Air Force, https://www.nationalmuseum.af.mil/Visit/Museum-Exhibits/Fact-Sheets/Display/Article/195925/gambit-1-kh-7-film-recovery-vehicle/

[165] National Reconnaissance Office, https://www.nro.gov/About-NRO/history/more-historical-programs/

[166] National Museum of the United States Air Force, https://www.nationalmuseum.af.mil/Visit/Museum-Exhibits/Fact-Sheets/Display/Article/195921/hexagon-kh-9-reconnaissance-satellite/

[167] National Reconnaissance Office, https://www.nro.gov/Portals/65/documents/history/csnr/gambhex/Docs/GAM_1_Fact_sheet.pdf

[168] The National Reconnaissance Office, https://www.nro.gov/About-nro/history/more-historical-programs

[169] National Air and Space Museum, https://airandspace.si.edu/explore/topics/space/space-shuttle-program

[170] Gamillo, E. (2023). "From Space to Museum Showcase: the Shuttles' Final Mission." Astronomy. https://www.astronomy.com/space-exploration/from-space-to-museum-showcase-the-space-shuttles-final-mission/

[171] National Aeronautics and Space Administration, https://www.nasa.gov/humans-in-space/nasa-day-of-remembrance-pays-tribute-to-fallen-astronauts/

[172] Defense Advanced Research Projects Agency (DARPA), https://www.darpa.mil/about-us/timeline/have-blue

[173] U.S. Air Force, https://www.af.mil/About-Us/Fact-Sheets/Display/Article/104482/b-2-spirit/

[174] Department of Defense, https://www.mda.mil/about/history.html; Department of State, http::2001-2009.state.gov/r/pa/ho/time/rd/104253.htm

[175] Frank Strickland, "The Early Evolution of the Predator Drone," *Studies in Intelligence* 57, no. 1 (2013): 1-6. https://www.cia.gov/static/Early-Evolution-of-Predator.pdf;_Defense Advanced

60

Research Projects Agency (DARPA), "Predator." https://www.darpa.mil/about-us/timeline/predator

[176] Roger Connor, "The Predator, a Drone That Transformed Military Combat," *National Air and Space Museum*, March 9, 2018, https://airandspace.si.edu/stories/editorial/predator-drone-transformed-military-combat

[177] Defense Advanced Research Projects Agency, "Predator." https://www.darpa.mil/about-us/timeline/predator; Strickland, "The Early Evolution of the Predator Drone," 1-6; Roger Connor, "The Predator, a Drone That Transformed Military Combat," *National Air and Space Museum*, March 9, 2018, https://airandspace.si.edu/stories/editorial/predator-drone-transformed-military-combat

[178] Defense Advanced Research Projects Agency, "Predator." https://www.darpa.mil/about-us/timeline/predator

[179] Ibid.

[180] Predator RQ-1/MQ-1/MQ-9 Reaper, *Air Force Technology*, https://www.airforce-technology.com/projects/predator-uav/; Christian Clausen, "The evolution of the combat RPA," *Air Force*, December 17, 2016, https://www.af.mil/News/Article-Display/Article/1032544/the-evolution-of-the-combat-rpa/

[181] DARPA, https://www.darpa.mil/About-Us/timeline/predator; U.S. Air Force, https://af.mil/About-Us/Fact-Sheets/Display/Article/104469/mq-1b-predator

[182] Predator RQ-1/MQ-1/MQ-9 Reaper, *Air Force Technology*, https://www.airforce-technology.com/projects/predator-uav/; Strickland, "The Early Evolution of the Predator Drone," 1-6.

[183] Christian Clausen, "The evolution of the combat RPA," *Air Force*, December 17, 2016, https://www.af.mil/News/Article-Display/Article/1032544/the-evolution-of-the-combat-rpa/

[184] John R. Hoehn and Paul R. Kerr, "Unmanned Aircraft Systems: Current and Potential Programs," *Congressional Research Service*, Report R47067, https://crsreports.congress.gov/product/pdf/R/R47067

[185] U.S. Air Force, "MQ-9 Reaper." https://www.af.mil/About-Us/Fact-Sheets/Display/Article/104470/mq-9-reaper/; John R. Hoehn and Paul R. Kerr, "Unmanned Aircraft Systems: Current and Potential Programs," *Congressional Research Service*, Report R47067. https://crsreports.congress.gov/product/pdf/R/R47067

186 U.S. Air Force, "MQ-9 Reaper," https://www.af.mil/About-Us/Fact-Sheets/Display/Article/104470/mq-9-reaper/

187 Ibid.

188 Ibid.

189 U.S. Air Force, "MQ-9 Reaper," https://www.af.mil/About-Us/Fact-Sheets/Display/Article/104470/mq-9-reaper/; Predator RQ-1/MQ-1/MQ-9 Reaper UAV, *Air Force Technology*, https://www.airforce-technology.com/projects/predator-uav/

190 U.S. Department of Defense, "Air Force to Retire MQ-1 Predator Drone, Transition to MQ-9 Reaper," https://www.defense.gov/News/News-Stories/Article/Article/1095612/air-force-to-retire-mq-1-predator-drone-transition-to-mq-9-reaper/; Predator RQ-1/MQ-1/MQ-9 Reaper UAV, *Air Force Technology*, https://www.airforce-technology.com/projects/predator-uav/

191 U.S. Air Force, https://www.nationalmuseum.af.mil/Visit/Museum-Exhibits/Fact-Sheets/Display/Article/195774/lockehhed-martin-rq-3-darkstar/; https://www.airandspace.si.edu/collection-objects/lockheed-martin-boeing-rq-3a-dark-star/nasm_A20070230000; https://www.armypress.army.mil/Portals/7/combat-studies-institute/csi-books/OP37.pdf

192 Ibid.

193 Ibid.

194 Lockheed Martin, "Popular Science Awards Lockheed Martin F-35 Lightning II and Polecat UAV Best of What's New for 2006." https://investors.lockheedmartin.com/node/17136/pdf; "From the Skunk Works, a New Polecat Emerges," *Air & Space Forces Magazine*, https://www.airandspaceforces.com/1005polecat/

195 Ibid.

196 U.S. Air Force, "RQ-170 Sentinel." https://www.af.mil/About-Us/Fact-Sheets/Display/Article/2796993/rq-170-sentinel/

197 Ibid.

[198] John R. Hoehn and Paul R. Kerr, "Unmanned Aircraft Systems: Current and Potential Programs," *Congressional Research Service*, Report R47067. https://crsreports.congress.gov/product/pdf/R/R47067

[199] Ibid.

[200] John R. Hoehn and Paul R. Kerr, "Unmanned Aircraft Systems: Current and Potential Programs," *Congressional Research Service*, Report R47067. https://crsreports.congress.gov/product/pdf/R/R47067; U.S. Air Force, "RQ-4 Global Hawk." https://www.af.mil/About-Us/Fact-Sheets/Display/Article/104516/rq-4-global-hawk/; U.S. Army https://www.armyupress.army.mil/Portals/7/combat-studies-institute/csi-books/OP37.pdf